Better Homes and Gardens®

LANDSCAPING AND OUTDOOR LIVING

Excerpted from Better Homes and Gardens® *COMPLETE GUIDE TO GARDENING*

BETTER HOMES AND GARDENS® BOOKS

Editor: Gerald M. Knox
Art Director: Ernest Shelton
Managing Editor: David A. Kirchner
Editorial Project Managers: Liz Anderson, James D. Blume,
   Marsha Jahns

Associate Art Directors: Linda Ford Vermie,
   Neoma Thomas, Randall Yontz
Assistant Art Directors: Lynda Haupert, Harijs Priekulis,
   Tom Wegner
Graphic Designers: Mary Schlueter Bendgen, Mike Burns,
   Brian Wignall
Art Production: Director, John Berg;
   Associate, Joe Heuer;
   Office Manager, Michaela Lester

President, Book Group: Jeramy Lanigan
Vice President, Retail Marketing: Jamie L. Martin
Vice President, Administrative Services: Rick Rundall

BETTER HOMES AND GARDENS® MAGAZINE
President, Magazine Group: James A. Autry
Editorial Director: Doris Eby
Editorial Services Director: Duane L. Gregg
Garden and Outdoor Living Editor: Douglas A. Jimerson
   Associate Editor: Jane Austin McKeon

MEREDITH CORPORATION OFFICERS
Chairman of the Executive Committee: E. T. Meredith III
Chairman of the Board: Robert A. Burnett
President: Jack D. Rehm

Landscaping and Outdoor Living
Contributing Project Editor: David Walsh
Editorial Project Manager: Liz Anderson
Graphic Designer: Randall Yontz
Contributing Editor: Jane Austin McKeon
Electronic Text Processor: Paula Forest

CONTENTS

THE GREAT OUTDOORS

Whether you seek a spot where you find solitude or a place to entertain a crowd, the solution to both needs can be as close as your own yard—with the right landscaping. By using your space wisely, it's possible, too, to set aside a play area, find room for vegetable and flower beds, screen out the view of a neighbor, perk up a streetside entry, and much, much more. In short, enjoying the great outdoors can be as easy as just stepping outside your house. All it takes are some great ideas plus a plan of action. And for those, just turn the page.

Put Your House in Proper Setting

The first impression a home gives is greatly governed by the landscaping in front. Ideally, the streetside entrance should be simply planned and planted. It should enhance, not overpower, the home's architecture.

A landscaped entry can erase the bareness of a new home or revitalize the looks of an older one. Before the front of this home (below) was redesigned, "unkempt" and "outdated" were the only ways to describe its exterior.

The lawn was sparse from years of poor maintenance and neglect. And, a jungle-like tangle of rangy, overgrown shrubs grew along the foundation of the house. Too scraggly to be salvaged, the lawn and all shrubs were ripped out. Only the trees—ash, maple, and oak—remain from the original landscape. New plantings include liriope, holly, and azalea. New sod carpets the yard, and flower borders brighten a visitor's approach.

A low stucco wall and wrought-iron gates create a side courtyard.

Once lacking luster, this bungalow now has a shining personality. New shrubs and lawn replaced scraggly predecessors, improving the home's outlook.

Outdoor Living

A well-planned outdoor living area offers privacy, comfort, and convenience—and beckons a home's occupants outside.

Decks, benches, and other functional structures form the framework. Trees, shrubs, and flowering plants add beauty.

The most livable decks and patios are hidden from the neighbors' view and secluded by shrubs, small trees, fences, or screens.

This small suburban backyard (below) was transformed into a haven for after-hours relaxation. Before the deck and spa were installed, the homeowners seldom used the cramped backyard because of its exposure and closeness to neighbor-

ing houses. Now the family just about moves outdoors for summer.

To tackle the privacy problem, the family opted for a small courtyard off the house instead of an open deck floating into the lawn. Screens and low walls at strategic points offer privacy. A nearby ash tree gives a leafy canopy for shade and adds a natural feeling of security to the setting.

Nearness to neighbors needn't mean forgoing privacy. Screens around the spa, strategic low walls, and an ash tree provide an intimate setting.

Gardens: None Too Small

"Miniatures" have long been favorites in art, flowers, even pets. A tiny garden, too, can have greater effect than its large counterpart. Its small size makes it easier to care for, too. Don't overlook front, back-, or side yards for refreshing compact gardens.

Too little space need not stop you from creating a restful haven of green or a colorful, blossom-filled retreat. Small areas mean lawns (and the resulting upkeep) are nearly out of the question, so pave or deck most of the surface. Leave some spots open for flowering plants, trees, shrubs, or climbing vines to soften stark lines of constructed privacy screens and fences.

Even a sloping, narrow yard can become a garden retreat. This San Francisco backyard (left) once was the play area for the homeowners' children. When the children grew up, the homeowners decided it was time for the backyard to grow up, too. They built a semicircular brick retaining wall and patio to hold back the hill. An adjacent deck expands the outdoor living area.

Compact gardens, like this sitting garden (opposite, top), often provide more punch to the viewer's eye than larger gardens. Despite its elaborate looks, the garden is low maintenance. There's no lawn to mow, and the raised brick beds make gardening chores, such as planting and weeding, easier on the gardener's back.

The garden also offers season-long changes in blooms and greenery. The center circle and two smaller beds are packed with masses of Hidcote and Munstead lavender. Spaces in between feature

Once this yard was a playground for youngsters. Creative landscaping turned it into a garden retreat for adults.

lily, delphinium, yarrow, veronica, lythrum, allium, and chives.

Small gardens can fit into any architectural scheme, too, as this garden (below, left) shows. After working several years to restore his Victorian home to its original condition, the homeowner still wasn't satisfied. His home lacked a garden that fit into the Victorian theme.

The homeowner worked with a garden designer to correct the problem. The result: a charming garden complete with a winding brick path and flower beds. A privacy fence encloses the garden, and perennials, annuals, roses, and bulbs produce a progression of color.

Even pocket-size spaces can pack a wallop with proper landscaping. A small, hilly yard now is a formal garden and dining area (below, right). Its main planting bed is only 15x20 feet, yet holds the center of attention. Evergreen boxwood and seasonal flowers, such as tulips and cinerarias, form a bouquet of color. Snow-white sweet alyssum adds to the color scheme.

Although most small-lot gardens sit off kitchens, any room can benefit beautifully from a nearby garden. A previously ignored spot outside a window can become a soothing escape if part of the wall is replaced by French or sliding glass doors and a petite patio is constructed.

A good bit of the country comes to this city garden. Flowers and herbs abound in the postage-stamp-size backyard.

Capturing Victorian charm, this garden comes with sundial and bench.

A hilly yard now is a formal garden with a dining area.

Analyzing Your Lot

To help you focus on developing your landscape plan, we offer a sample house and landscaping concept, sketched at right and far right. Arrows indicate how to look at your property to arrive at the best decisions.

Transforming your lot into the landscape you want may seem overwhelming. It takes time but can be enjoyable. The sketch at right helps you start. In the illustration, note all assets, liabilities, and some general problems to consider when developing an overall landscape plan. Consider these features along with your likes and dislikes.

Analysis. Note these factors: direction of winter winds; direction and angle of morning and afternoon sun (who wants a patio that gets hot, late afternoon sun?); unlovely views of the neighbor's garage; a too-narrow drive from the street to garage front entrance; unattractive view of an apartment house located to the northwest of the house; proximity of lot line to neighbor's drive; direct view of the street from the living room; lack of privacy at the rear of house.

Some clear assets are a view of distant hills and an existing oak of an approximately ten-foot diameter shading area at the rear of the house, including the dining and kitchen areas.

Look at your lot plan in these terms and decide its particular assets and liabilities. They may not, of course, be identical to those described above. Make a careful list of

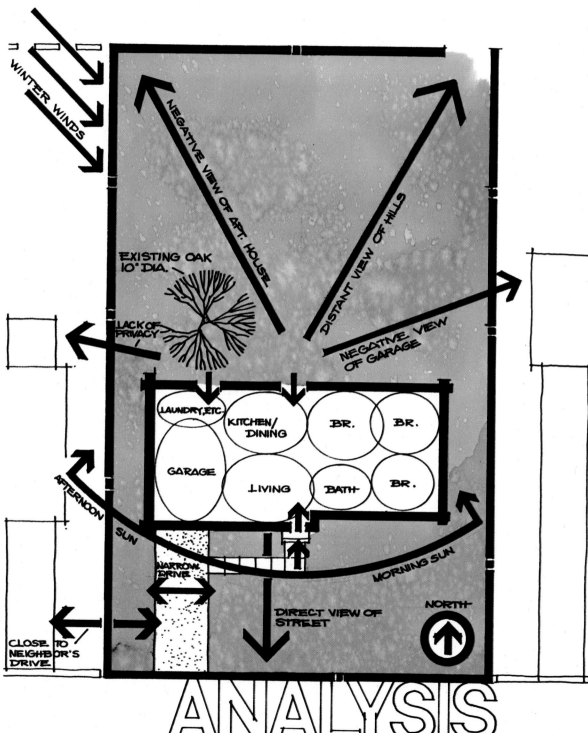

similar points that relate to your own house and surrounding property.

Concept. Compare, now, the sketch at left with the one at right to see what has been done to capitalize on the assets and minimize defects existing before a landscape plan was developed.

Notice that both structural and planting changes have been made. Plantings have accomplished more privacy for the front of the home from the street, as well as from the neighbor's property at left. Plantings also have helped to screen out the view of the neighbor's garage on the right, and of the more distant apartment house to the rear; they also protect against winter winds.

Structural changes have been used to widen the drive, partially to enclose play space, and to provide some separation and enclosure for outdoor living area. Enclosed work and storage space at the rear have been added in a convenient spot.

The shade of the oak tree has been used effectively by putting both play and outdoor living space at the rear of the house. To take advantage of the attractive view of hills, plantings near that edge of the lot have been kept low so they won't cut off the view.

Your good and bad points will be different from those in our plan, but you should find enough similarities to help you take the next step forward and, ultimately, arrive at solutions. And don't forget to accentuate your assets.

Make tentative alterations on the plan of your existing property, using both structural and plant changes to see what solutions you create. There is often a choice of several answers. Don't settle for the first that comes to mind until you have compared it with alternatives.

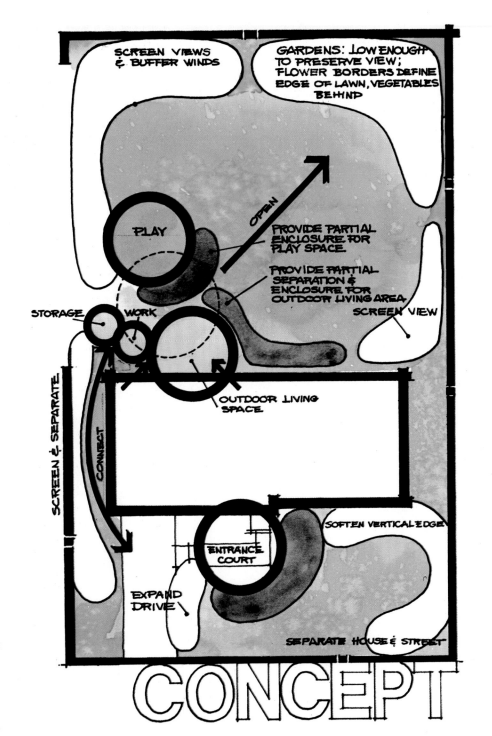

SCREEN VIEWS & BUFFER WINDS

GARDENS: LOW ENOUGH TO PRESERVE VIEW; FLOWER BORDERS DEFINE EDGE OF LAWN, VEGETABLES BEHIND

OPEN

PLAY

PROVIDE PARTIAL ENCLOSURE FOR PLAY SPACE

PROVIDE PARTIAL SEPARATION & ENCLOSURE FOR OUTDOOR LIVING AREA

SCREEN VIEW

STORAGE   WORK

SCREEN & SEPARATE

CONNECT

OUTDOOR LIVING SPACE

SOFTEN VERTICAL EDGE

ENTRANCE COURT

EXPAND DRIVE

SEPARATE HOUSE & STREET

CONCEPT

Making your own plan

Before you start to measure and draw a plan for your dream landscape, such as the one on the facing page, check to see if a plan of the house is already available. Can it be obtained from the builder or architect? If you used a Federal Housing Administration-insured or Veterans Administration-guaranteed loan for your house, the local FHA or VA office may have a plan. Get a copy; it will save you time in developing garden plans that fit your house.

Secure a loan plat. Next, see if there is a loan plat with your deed; if not, it may be on file with the loan company or local office of the FHA.

Get a copy of this, too, because it shows lot lines drawn to scale, location of house on lot, drive, any other paved areas, all structures, easements, and so on—information you can transfer to your own drawing.

When you talk with the builder, architect, or FHA official, also ask whether there is topographical data on file. It may show grades and drainage.

By all means, find out where any underground water or power lines are located. Indicate on your plan, too, the placement of the septic tank and field.

Do you need a surveyor? If your lot is irregularly shaped, if your house has different levels or unusual angles, or if your lot is rough and hilly, you'd be wise to hire a qualified land surveyor. The firm could save you from making costly mistakes.

Their survey will show the exact sizes of both lot and house, indicate exact grades of walks, steps, walls, drives, and the ground itself. And they can locate accurately all trees and other features of the property.

Do-it-yourself surveying. If your lot is relatively small and level, you can easily be your own surveyor. By taking all the measurements yourself, you'll be well acquainted with all the features of your property.

Start with graph paper, such as that shown on the facing page. The one-inch squares are divided into smaller segments to give you ten small squares to the inch. The larger squares will represent ten feet on the ground—the smaller squares will be equivalent to one foot on the ground. After you have established the lot lines and the position of your house on the graph paper, it is a simple matter to measure from the corners of the house to locate and record accurately the various features (trees, walks, slopes) on the plan.

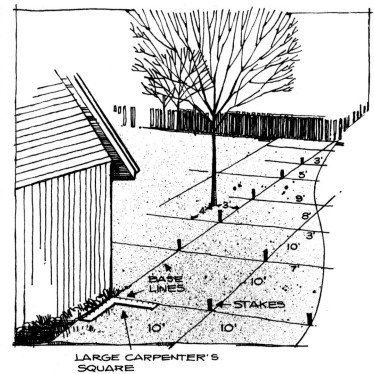

LARGE CARPENTER'S SQUARE

There are graph papers divided into several different numbers of squares, so if you find graphs divided into eight squares per inch, just have the larger squares on the graph represent eight feet on the ground. You may need to tape two graph pages together to get your entire lot drawn on it. Or you can put the backyard on one sheet and the front yard on another.

Take your ground measurements with a flexible 25- or 50-foot tape—one that winds up on a reel. It will come in handy later for laying out your plantings. Use a 12-inch ruler for aiding in the accurate recording of your measurements on the graph paper.

Measure carefully all around the outside of your house. Make a rough sketch as you go. Measuring to the nearest half-foot will do if you find smaller fractions difficult to translate to your lot. Plot all measurements you take on the graph paper and check to see that they agree.

Indicate door and window locations on the diagram; they will help later when you're ready to design plantings in relation to the house.

You are now ready to survey land around the house. Begin by measuring out from the corners of your house and projecting lines with stakes set at ten-foot intervals, as in the sketch above. These will be

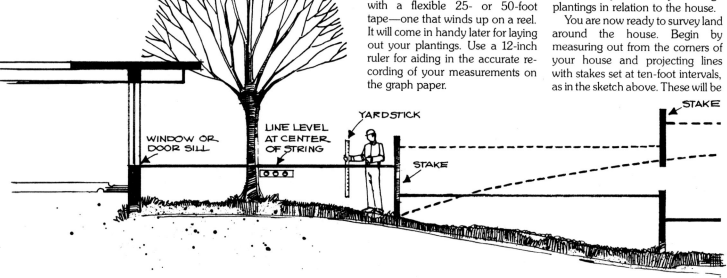

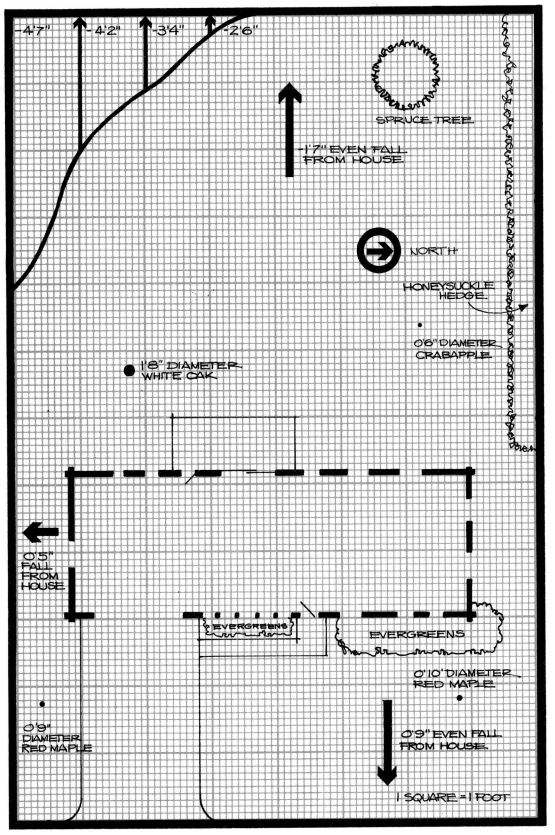

-4'7" -4'2" -3'4" -2'6"

SPRUCE TREE

-1'7" EVEN FALL FROM HOUSE

→ NORTH

HONEYSUCKLE HEDGE

0'6" DIAMETER CRABAPPLE

18" DIAMETER WHITE OAK

0'5" FALL FROM HOUSE

EVERGREENS

EVERGREENS

0'10' DIAMETER RED MAPLE

0'9" DIAMETER RED MAPLE

0'9" EVEN FALL FROM HOUSE

1 SQUARE = 1 FOOT

the base lines for your survey.

Next, measure from the base lines at right angles, running out to the points on your property lines, (as illustrated at the top of the opposite page).

If all your property lines are straight, just locate lot corners. If you plot base lines on the graph paper, measure from them to lot corners and draw lot lines onto the plan by connecting the corners.

Curved lot lines. Locate curved lot lines by measuring to a number of points off your base line. Be certain that all your measurements are made at right angles to base lines, from points set along the base line by your stakes.

Next, draw walks, drives, walls, fences, and all other structures on your lot plan. Seeing their relationship in the form of a diagram will help you visualize what you'll want to add or change later.

You also can locate the top and bottom of all terrace slopes by measuring from the base lines (as sketched at the bottom of the facing page). To avoid extra distance by measuring uphill or down on sloping property, use stakes at intervals and stretch a taut cord between them. Check with a level to be certain the cord is always in a horizontal position.

Additional tips on measuring grades are included on the following pages. If your property is sharply sloped, you might be wise to hire a professional surveyor.

Determine what to save. Once your plan includes all the information about existing plants and buildings, it is time to decide what to save, what to move, and what to remove completely. At this stage, even if you've decided not to hire a landscape architect to do the entire job, you still may wish to hire one on a "consultation only" basis. You'll get the most for your money if you do have a plot plan on which you can make notes of his or her professional advice.

If your family includes children, let them participate in making your basic plan and in considering what is to be changed or added. If they feel they have a part in planning, count on them to feel more interested in future care.

Grading Slopes for Correct Drainage

To determine any needed changes in grade, you can use a simple level or a precisely calibrated model, like the kind used by a professional builder. Your measurements should be as accurate as possible, but they need not be to the closest fraction of an inch.

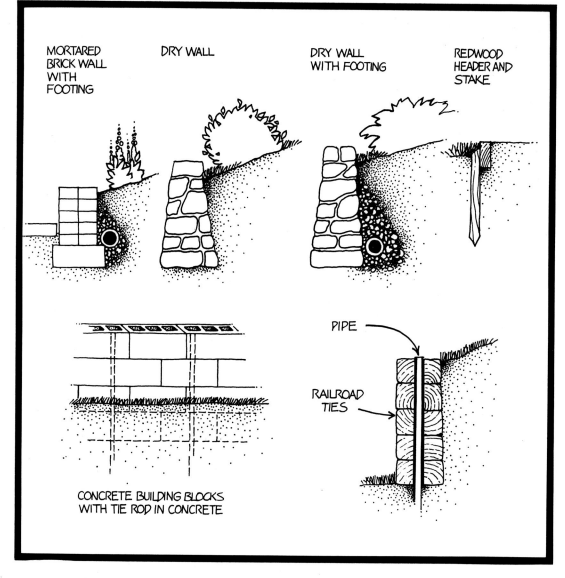

You can determine elevation by using a carpenter's level or string level and string. Here's how: Tightly stretch the string horizontally, from floor level to any point you wish. Make sure the string is horizontal by holding the carpenter's level along it (or by using a string level). Now measure up or down to that point to find the difference in grade. Add or subtract this from the floor grade of 100,000 feet to figure the relative elevation.

If grade changes are rapid or steep, you may have to stretch string at a higher or lower level in several steps. From this survey, you should be able to tell such factors as whether you need one or two steps, whether you'll have to install drainage tile, and where you must make grade changes.

When you have to change steep slopes, it is generally less expensive and more attractive to use retaining walls than to fill or excavate to achieve a more gentle slope. Walls may be of stone, brick, or concrete block—depending on which best suits your home's architectural style. Railroad ties also are used widely to solve the problems caused by a steeply sloping lot.

Retaining walls can enhance your landscape. But if the height needed exceeds four feet, don't try to install the wall yourself. Doing so requires both expert knowledge and professional equipment. Get a pro for a job of this scope.

If you've noticed a retaining wall leaning forward at its base, you are probably looking at the work of an amateur unfamiliar with nature's quirks. That person is apparently unaware that when soil is saturated, it exerts strong pressure on any restraining structure.

"Weep" holes at intervals in a wall are sometimes able to solve the problem, but, usually, the best long-range solution is to install a drainpipe. Set the pipe in a bed of loose aggregate or pebbles, behind the wall at its foot. Make sure the end of the pipe opens where water can run off without causing erosion problems to the surrounding areas.

Pictured above are a number of suggestions for solving drainage problems by using retaining walls.

Probably the easiest retaining walls for an amateur to install is either a dry rock wall (laid without mortar) or one made with railroad ties. Both let soil water escape through cracks, thus avoiding a buildup of water pressure—and all the problems that come with it.

These and other retaining walls are least troublesome if they're installed at a slightly backward slant—three inches to every vertical foot of wall. Walls that are to remain truly vertical must have concrete footings, loose aggregate fill, drainage pipes, or tiles.

If the installation of your wall requires excavating, be sure you plan to set the good topsoil to one side; then replace it on top the new grade you have formed. If sod is good, it, too, should be removed with care, rolled up, and relaid where needed.

If you decide to use "fill" soil to correct a steep slope, you'll get best results if you make a series of sup-

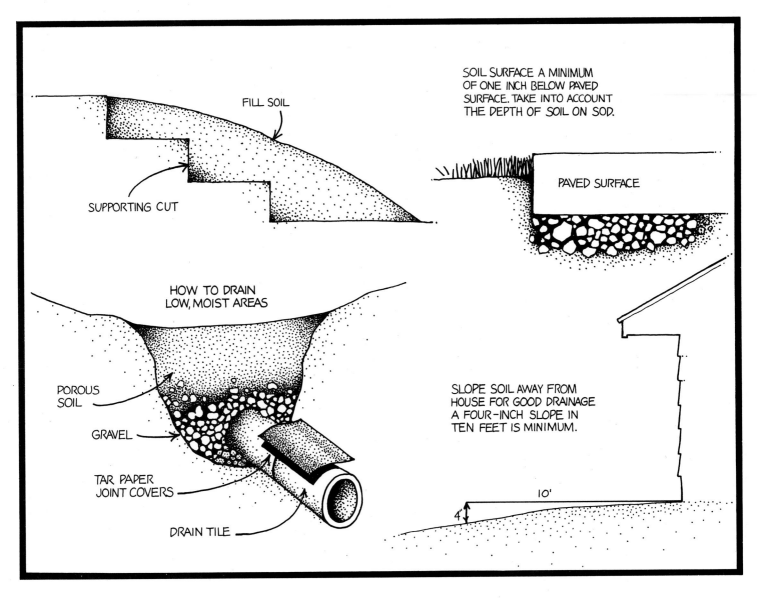

FILL SOIL

SUPPORTING CUT

SOIL SURFACE A MINIMUM OF ONE INCH BELOW PAVED SURFACE. TAKE INTO ACCOUNT THE DEPTH OF SOIL ON SOD.

PAVED SURFACE

HOW TO DRAIN LOW, MOIST AREAS

POROUS SOIL

GRAVEL

TAR PAPER JOINT COVERS

DRAIN TILE

SLOPE SOIL AWAY FROM HOUSE FOR GOOD DRAINAGE A FOUR-INCH SLOPE IN TEN FEET IS MINIMUM.

10'

4'

porting cuts (as shown in the sketch above, top left). This holds fill soil and makes it less subject to erosion before grass or ground cover becomes well established and can keep soil in place.

Make sure the area of soil close to the house slopes away to get good drainage. A four-inch slope in ten feet is minimum if you are to avoid water seeping into the foundation and basement.

The survey you made when you began to plan tells the exact slope. Check whether you need to make any changes in grade. A lawn that slopes as much as three feet horizontally to each vertical foot may be

safely mowed. Slopes steeper than that could be dangerous to mow.

In all cases where you have used fill to bring an area up to the level required for installing paved surfaces, remember that the new soil surface must be no less than one inch below a paved surface. Also, be sure to take into consideration the depth of soil on adjacent sod.

Diversion gutters provide a good way to drain low, moist areas. Such gutters keep moisture from your house and prevent rain from eroding surrounding soil. Dig a shallow trench six to eight inches wide and deep. Put an inch of gravel in the bottom of the trench, then lay drain

tile in place, using tar paper to cover the joints.

Now fill with several more inches of gravel before adding porous soil (add peat moss to soil if it's high in clay) to a level just below the former soil surface. Relay the sod you saved when you began excavating.

Before laying the gutter, note where the drainage tile will empty. It should run onto a flat, sodded area or harmlessly into a sewer.

Don't overlook the alternatives of using plants to solve problems caused by hillside slopes. Shrubs such as dwarf barberry and creeping juniper are favorites for keeping the slope of a graded terrace from erod-

ing. Combine them with some spring-flowering bulbs and with low-growing annuals for seasonal color on the slope. A vast array of ground covers can provide color and texture while holding soil to prevent erosion.

Rock gardens are another good way to tame a hillside. You can change an ugly bank into a major asset this way. Rocks must be secured to the bank by embedding the largest portions, leaving the smaller portions exposed. This requires a lot of work, but is worth it because you'll have a low-maintenance slope. The soil below must be porous for a garden to work well.

Choosing Plants

Once you've decided where to place the plants, you still need to choose the right plants for the right place. You'll want variety in size, texture, color, and growth habit. Be sure the plants will be healthy in the spots where you put them.

Since they grow slowly and take time to fill out, **shade trees** should receive your attention first. Set them out as soon as possible, especially if you plan to do your landscaping in stages over a number of years. That way, the young trees will grow while you proceed with the lesser elements in the landscape. Also, plan their placement in your yard carefully, remembering that the small trees you plant now will someday be much larger.

Many state agricultural colleges and county extension offices have informative booklets listing shade trees suited to the soil and climate of your area. They will tell you about growth rates, heights at maturity, density of shade, and other factors you need to know when comparing trees for selection.

If there's an arboretum nearby, visit it. You'll see mature trees there, all labeled, that also will help you decide. In addition, visit several nurseries, if possible. Compare prices, and you will discover they're based largely on the diameter of the tree. "Whips," or young unbranched trees, often sold bare-rooted, will cost little, but you'll have a long wait for shade. A tree four inches in diameter will cost a great deal more, but it will provide shade more quickly. And you can speed the growing time, only after the first year, by fertilizing around young trees in the fall or spring.

If you buy a good-size tree, let the nursery plant it. The extra money is well spent. The nursery's staff knows how to do least damage to the roots and how to set the tree in place. A reputable nursery also will offer a guarantee usually not given if you do the work yourself.

Trees such as maples, oaks, and beeches can grow to heights of 60 feet or more. Unless your property is large, don't use too many of these shade trees or you will diminish the importance of smaller ornamental trees that also can play an important and colorful role in your plan. Also, too many tall trees will shade your lot too much, resulting in poor growing conditions for shrubs, plants, small trees, and your lawn.

Evergreens, such as pines, firs, and spruces, will not grow as tall as oaks and other large shade trees, nor will they spread out as much. But, their conical form offers interesting contrast to deciduous trees. Plus, they remain green throughout the year, another point in their favor if they become part of your overall landscaping plan.

Young evergreens are commonly sold as "container-grown" plants and can safely be planted as a do-it-yourself project. However, be sure to ask your nursery for planting advice. After planting them, water young evergreen trees frequently during the first few years, unless rainfall is heavy. It's important that all evergreens—shrubs as well as trees—go into winter well-watered for them to survive, especially if autumn has been dry.

When feeding evergreens, always use a fertilizer formulated just for conifers, and use it only in amounts recommended. Their tender roots burn easily.

Ornamentals include a huge selection of trees and shrubs that do not grow much higher than the first story of a house, or, through consistent pruning, can be held at that height. Redbud, dogwood, saucer magnolia, flowering crab, and Japanese maple are only a few good choices on the list, depending on your growing zone and the effect you wish to create. Most need full sun for the best effect and color, so keep this in mind as you plan where to place them in your yard.

Evergreen shrubs deserve a place in your landscape for their contrast to deciduous shrubs and for their year-round green foliage. Several varieties of arborvitae, holly, juniper, yew, and pines, such as mugo, in the correct place, need little care in return for years of beauty.

Ground covers, lovely lifesavers in spots where shade is too deep for grass or where mowing is difficult, also fill an important role in landscape plans. Among those performing well in shade are vinca, ajuga, English ivy, pachysandra, and creeping thymes that send up a spicy scent when you walk on them.

Lawns must be chosen according to area. But no matter what grass seed you use, a lawn is an important element of the landscape because it offers a welcome, smooth contrast to other plants. As a gem gleams against a dark velvet setting, so shrubs, trees, and other plants are more interesting when set against the background supplied by the expanse of your lawn.

Flowers can play a big seasonal part in a landscape plan, but remember, if low maintenance is a major goal, you'll be wise to limit the space given to them.

Notice, at the bottom of this page, the key signs used in the sample landscape plan (opposite). They are symbols for ground cover, evergreen trees, evergreen shrubs, deciduous shrubs, overstory shade trees, understory ornamental trees, lawns, and flowers.

Use a sheet of tissue paper and colored pencils to draw similar symbols on your chart. This makes it easier to visualize the results on your lot. Compare your chart with the plan pictured on the opposite page. Does it have a comparable distribution and mixture of the various plant materials: trees for shade and ornament, evergreen trees and shrubs, deciduous shrubs, ground cover, lawn, and flowers? If not, do you want to change your plan—perhaps eliminate or add some plants?

Beginners tend to overplant because it is difficult for them to gauge how much plants are going to grow during the years to come. Check references about specific plants to see if you've allowed enough space for the growth of shrubs and trees over a ten-year period.

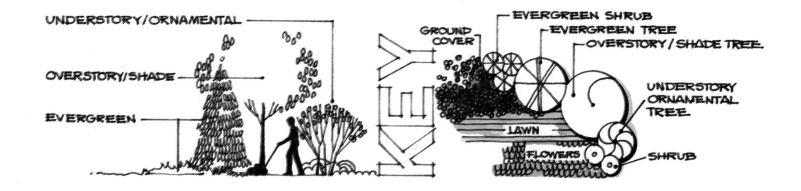

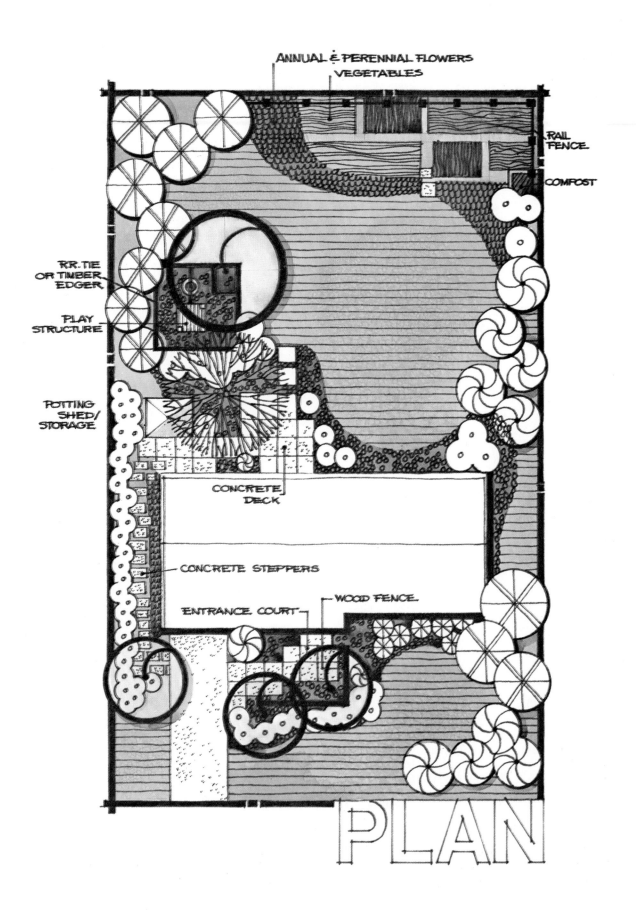

ANNUAL & PERENNIAL FLOWERS
VEGETABLES

RAIL FENCE

COMPOST

RR.TIE OR TIMBER EDGER

PLAY STRUCTURE

POTTING SHED/ STORAGE

CONCRETE DECK

CONCRETE STEPPERS

WOOD FENCE

ENTRANCE COURT

PLAN

Where to Plant Trees

Trees offer irreplaceable charm and character to a home. Plant them in poorly chosen locations, though, and they can lose their appeal as they mature. Follow these few easy guidelines when landscaping your property.

Because trees contribute to the enjoyment of your home, their placement and care are important. Failure to place trees in the right spots when they're young can lead to disappointment years later when growth begins to show a mistake was made. But by then it's usually too late to do much about it without a lot of work.

Each tree variety has its own spacing and growth requirements. That's why it's wise to consult with a tree nursery staff before purchasing a new tree for your lawn.

In general, trees reaching a height of 20 feet or more should be planted at least 15 feet from any structure to keep their roots away from the foundation. Never plant such a tree near utility lines or under a roof overhang. Otherwise, you'll have to keep it severely trimmed, ruining its natural shape.

Shade trees. With shade trees, keep in mind the direction and angle of the sun as you plan a location for planting. Before you start digging, select a spot where the tree will provide adequate shade where you need it. Locate trees to frame the house, choosing those that will stay in scale with the size of your home and its architectural features.

There are different types of shade trees, each offering unique shading characteristics.

Pyramidal-shaped trees (for example, pin oak, small-leaved linden, and red horse chestnut) are ex-

cellent for placement on lawns or along streets. They must be spaced widely to permit light to penetrate beneath them so grass will not be shaded out. Avoid planting them directly in front of windows. Their dense foliage will hide the home and block the view.

Weeping shade trees (such as beech, willow, and European ash) need open spaces, too. Typically, they spread as wide as they are tall. Most city lots will accommodate only smaller weeping shade trees.

Vase-shaped trees (such as red and white oak, sugar maple, and sycamore) grow tall, with top branches spreading somewhat wider than bottom ones. They make wonderful backyard trees where lots of shade is needed. However, too many vase-shaped trees in a small area will make it difficult to keep a lawn looking good because of the lack of sunlight.

Rounded trees, such as red maple, hawthorns, and serviceberry, on the other hand, cause few problems for lawns. Their branching makes them suitable for planting along streets. They also make beautiful front lawn specimens.

Columnar trees (gray birch, white poplar, and Lombardy poplar) are tall and slender. They're excellent when planted close together along a property line to screen the view and provide a windbreak.

Small flowering trees, such as crab apples and redbuds, are beautiful as ornaments and useful as boundary trees. They also are favorites for planting near walks or patios because their root systems aren't very vigorous and won't split the concrete. Plant them on lot corners and with flowering borders—their shade doesn't interfere with the growth of most flowers. Most flowering trees can be placed within eight feet of your house.

Conifers. Before buying one of the many varieties of pine, spruce, fir, cypress, or hemlock, check with the staff at your nursery to see what the shape and size of a mature tree will be. Needle evergreens, such as large pine and spruce, will "outgrow the house" if planted too close. Keep them at least 20 feet in front and 20 feet to the side of your house so they don't interfere.

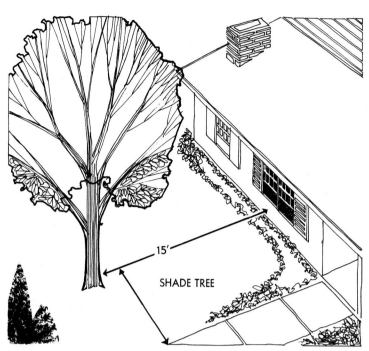

If the height of a tree will exceed 20 feet when mature, plant it at least 15 feet from the house or other buildings. For very large trees, double this spacing. Shade trees should be planted at least ten feet from walks, drives, and patios so their roots won't break up the surfacing.

Keep the shade "target" in mind as you locate trees. For afternoon shade in the summer, plant trees ten to 15 feet south and 20 feet west of the target area. If the tree will grow to be large, increase the distance away from the base in both directions. Take care not to plant tall-growing trees under power or telephone lines.

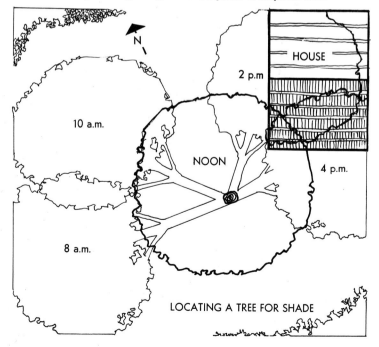

LOCATING A TREE FOR SHADE

FOUNDATION PLANTING

Locate foundation plantings carefully. Be sure you know how large they will be when full-grown. If you're trying to fill a barren area, don't overplant to fill the space. Give shrubs and trees adequate room to grow naturally without crowding. Allow three feet between the house and trunks for most shrubs; spreading junipers should have four feet.

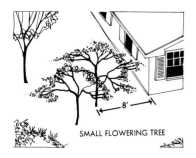

SMALL FLOWERING TREE

Dwarf-type fruit trees and other small flowering trees are ideal for small lots because you can plant them fairly close together without interfering with other gardening. Allow about ten feet between trees (or enough distance so their branches just touch—not entwine—when mature) and at least eight feet from your house.

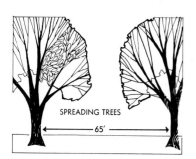

SPREADING TREES

Large trees with wide-spreading branches—for example, linden, silver maple, and sweet gum—need at least 65 feet between trunks. If they're closer than this, their branches eventually will entwine and block out the sun from the lawn or flowers below. Even if branches don't tangle, less-than-ideal spacing can mean trees will have uneven branching.

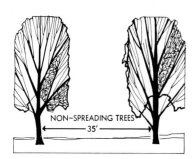

NON-SPREADING TREES

Non-spreading trees under 35 feet high (the hybrid maple, for instance) need 35 feet between trunks to show off their beautiful forms. Non-spreading trees with a narrow shade area, such as Bolleana poplar, don't need as much room allocated to them. For uniform growth among these non-spreaders, be sure to buy grafted stock.

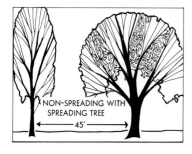

NON-SPREADING WITH SPREADING TREE

Non-spreading trees planted with spreading trees create a problem when the larger ones compete with the smaller for nutrients and light. Unless they're planted 45 feet apart (for example, a pin oak with a silver maple), the smaller tree will grow lopsided. If your landscape plan doesn't permit this much space, consider substituting shrubs for the small tree.

SAVE TREES WHEN CHANGING GRADES

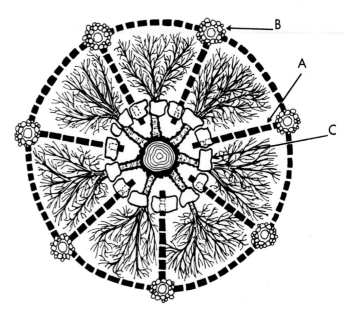

Provide proper drainage and air circulation for tree roots before adding topsoil to level a grade. Otherwise, the tree could suffocate. Spread tree food, then lay drainage tiles in spoke-wheel fashion (A) from trunk to drip line of outer branches. Add six-inch bell tile (B) wherever "spokes" meet perimeter. Use stone for wall (C) around trunk, starting two feet out, up to intended level.

(Side view of above procedure.) Before adding topsoil to level grade, cover ground-tile ducts (A) with coarse material such as rock, gravel, or stone, as shown. Add thin layer of hay, then pile topsoil to desired level. To prevent clogging, cover tile openings in tree well with stones. Cap bell tiles (B) with screen wire.

Good Planning Pays Off

The drawings on these two pages show the results of a good landscape plan: a home with surroundings that are truly enjoyable.

The right plantings—plus perhaps some structural alterations—can revitalize a house and make it more dramatic. Let's take a look at the samples sketched on these two pages to find out how all the changes can come together.

An ornamental shrub and ground cover in a rectangular planting area (above) make the front entrance attractive, plus add a bit of color when the flowers are in bloom. A low, partial fence and two ornamental trees lend privacy to the area. The two evergreens (extreme right) amplify the entry's private feeling by cutting off an undesirable direct view into living areas from the street in front. These trees will serve as a green privacy screen all year long.

The evergreens also help lessen the separation between indoors and out—another desirable goal be-

cause it gives the feeling of more living space.

Even the shape of the evergreens offers a landscaping advantage. Their conical form will generally cause less shading than spreading trees, letting more light into the home's living areas. If strung with lights, these same trees will make cheery decorations during the winter holidays.

In front of the entry fence and the ornamental trees, low-growing deciduous shrubs make a flowing transition between lawn and paved entry area. Flowering quince and dwarf barberry are two possible

choices for this spot. If you live in a temperate zone, you may prefer dwarf azaleas to add an accent of color in the spring. In either case, an interplanting of bulbs that flower in the spring would be attractive.

The rear of our sample house plan (opposite) is equally attractive and livable.

The concrete deck—with access from either the dining room or the kitchen-utility area—provides an ample outdoor living area for the whole family to enjoy. When grilling out, family cooks have quick access to kitchen supplies.

A potting shed and storage unit make it easy to put garden tools out of sight when not in use, plus shelter the stored items from the elements. Behind it, a partly enclosed play structure with adjacent play area will appeal greatly to the younger members of the family.

In installing the paved area, care was taken to leave enough open space around the shade tree at the rear of the house so it receives adequate moisture. If you surround a tree with large areas of paved surface, you are almost certain to lose the tree because vital moisture won't be able to reach its roots.

Remember, also, that if you've done any filling around a tree that you wish to save, you must install a "tree well" that permits the base of the tree to stay at its original soil level. (See page 19 for an illustration of a tree well.) The well should be a minimum of twice the diameter of the tree.

Additional plantings include a second shade tree to protect both play area and deck from the hot summer sun.

A small planting bed close to the house includes an ornamental tree and some ground cover. (Another option for a spot like this is to use flowering plants that do not need full sun.)

A grouping of understory ornamental trees (only one shows at lower left in this sketch) wipes out an undesirable view of the neighbor's garage and lends greater privacy to the entire rear area of the property.

Lawn reaching beyond the deck area should have a border with a mowing edge for easy maintenance. The border also helps to separate the lawn from adjacent beds of shrubs and ground cover.

If your family likes outdoor games, such as volleyball or badminton, be sure to include enough open lawn space. Try not to plant easily damaged shrubs or flowering plants near areas where they are almost certain to be tramped on as balls or birds are retrieved.

Seeing an artist's sketches makes it easy to visualize how a landscaping project will turn out. But what can you do to find out whether your proposed landscaping changes will have the effect you want? Try this: Take a black-and-white snapshot of the front of your house and have it enlarged to, say, 10x12 inches. Then use tissue paper to sketch the proposed plantings in the appropriate locations indicated on the landscape plan. Do this for both the front and the backyard.

If the results are not what you sought, move plantings on the paper until what you see pleases you and your family.

In addition, when you draw your plan on cross-sectioned paper, structural elements may not look as you had hoped they would. If that's so, change their location and height until the final product approximates the view you had in mind.

At this stage, even drastic alterations cost nothing but paper and time. Later, they may be expensive or impossible.

Front Entrances

Soften, cool, screen, define. Plants at the front of your home can have many purposes. As it blends with the neighborhood, your landscape arrangement also reflects your family's personality and style. Trees and shrubs can create an enchanting view or block a less pleasant one. The blunt lines of house corners, porches, and walls are soothed with flowing lines of well-placed greenery. Splashes of spring and fall color signal "welcome" to passersby. Trees help tame extremes in temperature by reducing heat glare and chilly winds.

Favorite landscape plants have balance and grace that outdo any sculpture. Yet almost nothing makes homeowners so nervous as deciding what to plant around the front of the family dwelling. The trees and shrubs set along a foundation are fairly permanent. Because this is true, wise selection is vital; correct choices can spell little maintenance and a pleasing arrangement for years to come.

Plants can contribute to the beauty of your home. They have a multitude of forms, textures, and colors. They also have characteristic lines determined by their trunks, stems, and branches.

But their value is far more than decorative. Some are downright practical, as well. Can they offer a screen for privacy or shade? Are there some that will reduce mainte-

nance problems? Can they mark off areas that reflect interests of family members—a garden patch, a play area complete with tire swing, a gracious rose showpiece, or a quiet place to sip lemonade and watch the birds?

The placement of many trees and shrubs can be ecologically sound, too. Plants can affect climate in limited areas. Cooling, parasol-like trees on the sunny side of the house can reduce strain on the air conditioner. Farm families have long known that a windbreak to slow wintry gales assists in conserving heat and restraining drifts. City folks are discovering this, as well, when they plan tree placement.

The color of trees and shrubs can make a yard appear cooler, too. Green and blue-green are cool; red, orange, and yellow are hot, advanc-

ing colors. Remember the changing seasons. Will the plants you chose for the focal point remain attractive through most of the year? Take care to select colors that coordinate with your home's paint or siding and with other plants.

Size, like color, can accent or overwhelm. That cute young shrub just under the living room window may one day grow tall and bushy, blocking your view. Set trees where they will frame the house. Select plants that will stay in scale with architectural features even when full-grown; avoid large plants near the entrance.

With new homes, put one or two fast-growing trees near the corners of the house. Slower-growing trees on other corners and along the back will be stately by the time the speedy ones start to deteriorate.

■ MONOTONOUS, UNIFORM PLANTINGS; SHRUBS WHICH GROW UP TO BLOCK VIEWS FROM WINDOWS; PLANTS WITH SEVERE UPRIGHT FORMS THAT CONFLICT WITH A HOUSE'S HORIZONTAL LINES.

AVOID

■ PLANT CHOICES WITH LITTLE REGARD FOR THEIR RELATIONSHIPS TO THE HOUSE; PLANTINGS THAT APPEAR SPARSE AND UNDERSIZED.

■ OVERFORMALITY--FORMALLY TRIMMED SHRUBBERY NOT WARRANTED BY STYLE OF HOUSE; TEDIOUS CARE; PLANTS NOT USED TO CREATE THE OUTDOOR SPACES, BUT RATHER AS ORNAMENTS FOR THE HOUSE.

■ DEVELOP THE LANDSCAPE PLAN AROUND IMPORTANT ASPECTS OF THE HOUSE. FOR EXAMPLE, FOCUS LANDSCAPE TREATMENT TOWARD CREATING A SHADED ENTRANCE. IN ALL PLANTINGS, CONSIDER THE SEASONAL QUALITIES OF PLANT MATERIAL: FLOWERS, FALL COLOR, WINTER COLOR, OR FORM.

INSTEAD

■ CREATE A NATURAL SETTING FOR THE HOUSE. INFORMAL PLANTINGS CAN SOFTEN ABRUPT BUILDING EDGES ALLOWING THE HOME TO BECOME PART OF THE LANDSCAPE. PLANTINGS WHICH RESEMBLE FIELD OR FOREST MAY ATTRACT BIRDS AND SMALL ANIMALS.

■ EXTEND HORIZONTAL BUILDING LINES AND SOFTEN ABRUPT VERTICAL EDGES BY USING MASSES OF PLANTS AT CORNERS. SUBTLE CHANGES IN THE TYPE AND HEIGHT OF PLANTS PRODUCE AN UNDULATING, APPEALING FRAME FOR THE HOUSE.

Patio Surfaces

When building a patio, choose surface materials with the exact texture and appearance you want. Your patio options are many: concrete slabs or concrete, stone, clay, bricks, tile, even wood. Or use a combination.

No matter what patio surface you prefer, you probably can do part or all of the work yourself. Select a surface that gives a "designer's touch" to your overall backyard landscaping.

Concrete. Always a popular choice for patios, concrete is a versatile surface because you can pour it in any shape and then give it a variety of finishes before it hardens. Stamping, scoring, brushing, exposing aggregate, and adding pigment are ways to take away the monotony of smooth concrete.

Concrete slabs. Buy them in a variety of surface textures and colors ready to lay, or make your own by pouring concrete into a form you've constructed from wood or metal. Patio blocks, which are normally about two inches thick, are laid on a bed of sand, gravel, or packed soil.

Flagstone, slate, bluestone. These expensive and beautiful textured surfacing materials are available in earthy colors, such as buff, yellow, reddish brown, and gray. Installing them to form a patio usually means mortaring them into place in a random, jigsaw-like pattern on a concrete bed.

Brick. Lay bricks on a bed of sand, securing them with additional sand brushed into the joints between bricks. Or set them in mortar on a bed of concrete. Select an interesting pattern for your patio (see sketches on the opposite page) and be sure to use long-wearing SW (Severe Weather) grade brick.

The knobby texture of concrete aggregate adds to the appeal of any outdoor setting.

Clay tile. A good choice—but expensive. Use quarry tile or patio tile, choosing from several different sizes, colors, and shapes.

Loose surfaces. Wood chips, bark, pea gravel, pebbles, or crushed rock generally are used in combination with other patio materials. Use them around trees and shrubbery or between slabs in a "stepping-stone" walkway. To prevent weed growth through the loose surface, lay a sheet of polyethylene film or building felt before spreading the aggregate. Contain perimeters with corrugated metal edging or with redwood 2x4s set on edge.

Construction tips

• Check local building codes and zoning ordinances before you start building your patio. Then, lay out a scaled version of your design on paper, marking the dimensions carefully. Use the drawing to figure the

Flagstone and pebbles create a simple patio under a shady catalpa tree.

amount of surfacing materials your new patio will require (a building materials supplier can help determine your needs). Keep the price you're willing to pay in mind as you make your plans—fancy flagstone or slate will be much more expensive to install than other materials, such as concrete or patio blocks.

• The next step is to stake out your

HERRINGBONE

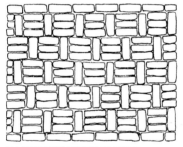

BASKET WEAVE VARIATION

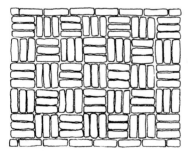

BASKET WEAVE (brick on edge)

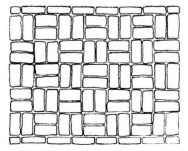

BASKET WEAVE (brick laid flat)

design and prepare the site. Depending on the terrain, you may have to remove terraces or high spots or bring in fill dirt for any low areas.

• The surface of a patio is usually even with the surrounding yard or slightly above it. That means you'll have to excavate six to eight inches to accommodate the patio's surface and base. To ensure proper drainage, a patio that is adjacent to a house should be sloped one-eighth to one-fourth inch per foot away from the house.

Prepare a two- to four-inch bed of fine gravel or sand before laying the patio. Be sure the bed is free from high or low spots.

If you want to set the surface material in mortar, pour an additional bed of concrete about four inches deep. Let it harden and cure before laying the patio.

Concrete pads give the illusion of spaciousness to this narrow lot.

This brick patio couldn't contain itself! It flows into curved brick pathways, and flower and vegetable beds.

Though this backyard is large, the homeowners opted for a compact deck to make gatherings feel intimate, and to leave space for lawn activities.

Decks

Build a deck to expand your home's living space. Then, you can move many of your favorite activities outside where you'll enjoy them in the fresh air.

What is a deck? It is an idyllic island for basking in the sun—your very own secluded corner for grabbing some well-deserved outdoor privacy without leaving home. And it's a great place to entertain your family and friends. When remodeling an older home, one of the best ways to increase property value is to add a deck.

You can build a deck to suit almost any terrain or setting. Use it to frame a pleasant view or to solve the landscaping problems posed by an odd-shaped yard. Attach a deck to your house and use it as a walk-out balcony to expand the second story. Or build a low, freestanding platform around the shady comfort of a big backyard tree. If your yard is on a slope, a deck will give you a much-needed level surface for many activities.

Then embellish your deck with weatherproof furniture and graceful accessories, such as potted plants and colorful outdoor cushions. Or

Conversations flow when friends gather on this deck with wraparound seating.

build in benches for extra seating and add a countertop and grill arrangement for barbecues and parties. If you prefer not to cover the entire deck, construct a small, roofed alcove at one end as a shady dining spot. Outdoor lighting is a plus, too.

Remember, build a deck for both privacy and comfort. You'll enjoy your deck more if you build it away from annoyances such as the neighbor children's play area, noisy street traffic, or a loud air conditioner. You might want to use dense shrubs or a constructed privacy fence to further reduce outside distractions.

Also, keep an eye on the sun. The north and east sides of a home are usually cool in the afternoon and evening, so they make good locations for a deck. Depending on climate, a deck facing west or south may get too warm during parts of the day.

Construction Tips

Building a deck is like any home improvement project—you need to plan carefully before beginning. Whether you design the deck yourself or call in a professional to do it for you, consider a few basics before you start.

• Check for restrictions in zoning and building codes. Do local zoning ordinances have a "setback" requirement specifying how far the deck must be removed from your property line? If so, it's a good idea to call in a surveyor before you start building. Also, if there's an easement in your property deed allowing for excavation on your lawn, you may want to avoid building in that area.

• Can you build all or part of the deck yourself? Of course! Most decks—even the more elaborate ones—are suitable projects for the average do-it-yourselfer. If you need help selecting materials, check with an employee at your local building supply outlet. If you need help with construction, you may want to hire a carpenter.

• To avoid the "added-on" look, be sure your deck blends with the design and color of your home. Decks constructed from garden-grade redwood or cedar can be left with a natural unstained look. With other woods, you'll want to stain or paint.

Perched on what was once a "slope without hope," a cantilevered deck moves entertaining to new heights.

Angled flooring and detailing on different floor levels keep this sprawling deck from looking too massive.

Shelters That Provide Shade

If the afternoon sun makes your deck or patio a little too hot to handle and you don't have a large shade tree handy, build an overhead canopy to take the heat off.

A structure designed to provide shade is an easy addition to most decks or patios. And the procedure is simple: **1.** Sink two, four, or more pressure-treated support posts in the ground below the frost line and set in concrete. Make sure they're perpendicular. **2.** Attach horizontal beams to the posts and, if necessary, to the house. **3.** Install your choice of canopy.

Depending on the amount of shade you want, you can choose from a variety of shelter treatments. For lots of shade, use tightly spaced lattice (lath strips, 1x2s, 2x2s, or the like) or even canvas. For filtered sunlight—enough light for many plants—space the roof treatment into a trellislike effect. Let vining plants climb and spread across the structure.

For a structure that lets in plenty of light, allow beams to be exposed or install a sun screen of widely spaced stringers reaching from beam to beam. Corrugated plastic laid across the beams makes a quick and easy shelter. Pitch the roof so rain and snow don't accumulate.

Use your imagination as you design this kind of structure. The construction doesn't have to be only functional. It can also be a dramatic addition to the architectural lines of your home. If the shelter is a canopy for an existing deck, match the materials as closely as possible, or restain the deck so it matches the new canopy.

Harmonizing well with a redwood deck, this small gazebo offers a family of four a shady spot for cool relaxation.

An open-air lath structure can offer privacy without blocking desired views.

Attaching a gazebo to the house saves valuable space in a tiny side yard.

An arbor and swing create the perfect setting for reading—or daydreaming.

Going out for dinner takes on a new meaning with a dining nook like this.

Gaining Privacy with Hedges

Privacy can be much simpler and lovelier than stone walls or a moat around your castle (or modest home). A hedge—whether formal or informal—can nicely separate your yard from the sights and sounds of the world around.

Choose tall, columnar evergreens, such as these pyramidal Chinese junipers, to soften a wall or hide an eyesore.

Whether in the suburbs with neighbors close to lot lines, in the city with a postage-stamp yard, or even in the country where farm buildings loom near the house, hedges can screen out eyesores, offer friendly separation from the folks next door, and join all the elements of your landscape design.

There's nothing new about using plants rather than a fence or wall for privacy. Almost 4,500 years ago, Egyptians grew natural screens, much like the ones we use today.

A hedge can be any continuous, close planting of trees, shrubs, even tall annual flowers. The plant you select depends on why you want the hedge. Some thorny choices provide a barrier almost as forbidding as a stone wall. Others cleverly distract the eye from an ugly air conditioner next to the neighbor's house or separate a home auto repair center from the patio.

A plant screen takes more space than a fence or wall, but it also has the advantage of color and texture variations. Some are also good insulators against noise and the lights of oncoming cars. If space is a problem, vines on fences or partitions of wood, brick, or plastic can be used as screens.

Evergreen shrubs provide privacy in winter better than deciduous shrubs and trees, but they don't offer the variety of twig and flower color you get with hedge plants such as forsythia and camellia.

Location is important when deciding between deciduous and evergreen hedges. Deciduous hedges might work just as well around a patio because they're at their leafy best when you're making most use of the patio.

Of the many shrubs available, some make better screens than others because they are denser. Heights will vary from region to region because of environmental conditions and the varieties of shrubs on the market. Check with a local nursery for recommendations for your area.

Central region shrubs	Height (in feet)
Amur privet	to 15
Common lilac	8–10

	Height (in feet)
Cranberry bush viburnum	8–10
French hybrid lilac	6–10
Japanese barberry	3–4
Japanese quince	5–7
Lynwood forsythia	5–8
Pfitzer juniper	6
Snowball bush	8–10
(*Viburnum plicatum*)	
Tatarian honeysuckle	to 10
Vanhouttei spirea	5–6
Warty barberry	3–4
Wayfaring tree viburnum	8–10

Southern region shrubs	Height (in feet)
Border privet	to 10
Camellia (*C. japonica*)	3–40
Camellia	2–8
(*C. sasanqua*)	
Crape myrtle	to 25
Flowering quince	to 5
Gardenia species, varieties	to 6
Hydrangea	5
(*H. macrophylla*)	
Oleander	to 20
Shrub althaea	to 12
(*Hibiscus syriacus*)	

Eastern region shrubs	Height (in feet)
Common box	to 25
Common lilac	10–20
Common privet	to 15
Japanese quince	to 10
Lynwood forsythia	8–10
Mock orange	4–8
Rose (*Rosa rugosa*)	to 6
Vanhouttei spirea	to 6
Winged euonymus	to 8

Western region shrubs	Height (in feet)
Abelia	to 6
Bridal-wreath spirea	4–8
(*S. prunifolia*)	
Camellia (*C. reticulata*)	to 30
Camellia (*C. sasanqua*)	to 30
Darwin's barberry	3–10
Dwarf Japanese yew	to 3
Hydrangea	to 10
(*H. paniculata*)	
Japanese flowering quince	3–6
Japanese holly	4–10
Japanese privet	6–10
Myrtle (*Myrtus communis*)	3–10

Screening your driveway

Cars may be a symbol of our lifestyle, but where we put them offers a challenge to landscape designers. The solution to the problem of off-street parking can be an asset to your home. The plants used can also help protect the car from summer heat and winter wind.

Here are three designs for an 85x60-foot property, each with a different solution. All plans were developed so they require minimum maintenance. The plants are keyed in the box below.

Right: The parking area cuts out a 24-foot strip from the property, reducing the lawn area that needs grooming. Small trees are used here and in the two other plans. The dog-

woods and hawthorns are clouds of white in spring; the broom is yellow. Imperial honey locusts cast a light shade over the parking area. The trees are deciduous but are not messy.

Below left: Parking space in this design provides enough room for you to swing your car around and head out to the street. Two white flowering crab apples (Katherine) and two pink ones (Hopa) form a spectacular blooming triangle, regardless of the viewing angle. Oregon holly grape has yellow flowers (to supplement the forsythia), followed by turquoise-blue berries.

Below right: An asphalt or gravel parking area is actually an extension of the street. It makes parking easy for a lot of cars—but check with local authorities before

building such a parking area. Landscaping here calls for more trees—to provide privacy and to screen the car space. The design is well adapted to a slightly sloping yard.

Don't settle too quickly on plain concrete or asphalt. Even the driveway and off-street parking area offer chances for introducing texture, col-

or, and pattern into your landscape. Dark paving retains heat late into a summer evening, warming cars parked on it. Deciduous trees can help keep cars and the area near the house cool.

To protect plantings along the driveway, install bumpers made from railroad ties or 2x4s.

Key to illustrations

Small trees	Height (in feet)	Shrubs	Height (in feet)
A Cutleaf staghorn sumac	5–10	**H** Warminster broom	3–6
B Crab apple, Hopa	6–10	**I** Cranberry cotoneaster	3–4
C Crab apple, Katherine	6–10	**J** Paxistima canbyi	8
D Dogwood, Chinese	10–12	**K** *Euonymus fortunei* 'acuta'	3–4
E Hawthorn 'Autumn Glory'	9–15	**L** Bigleaf winter creeper	2–4
F Honey locust 'Imperial'	30–40	**M** Lynwood forsythia	5–7
G White birch	20–35	**N** Oregon holly grape	2–4
		O Spreading cotoneaster	5–6
		P Beautybush	7–8

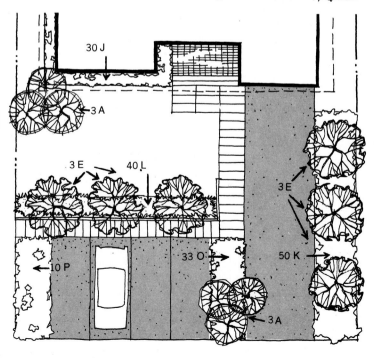

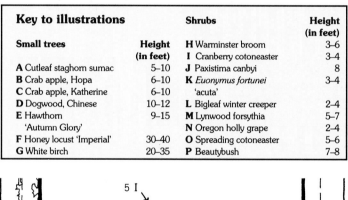

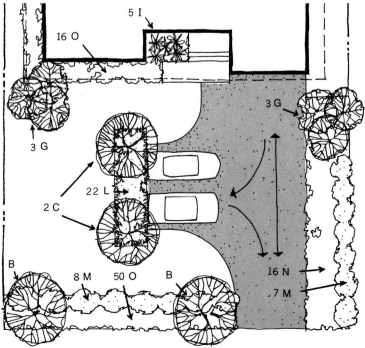

Privacy Fences

Your yard is one of the few places you can go for a little peace and quiet. So, why not screen it from the hustle and clatter of day-to-day living?

Constructing your own privacy fence is relatively easy. And it's a lot less expensive than buying and installing pre-built fence panels.

If you have a deck, extend its design by building your fence from similar materials in order to maintain a more unified landscaping appearance.

Or build a fence with its own character and make it a focal point of the yard. The design possibilities are infinite.

For example, look at the drawings (right). The first, a herringbone

pattern, uses 1x6 boards toenailed to a frame of 4x4 posts and 2x4 rails. The angular pattern is accentuated by half-inch spaces between the boards, which also allow sunlight to filter through.

The board-and-board design (upper right) offers an attractive horizontal line. The 1x8 boards are nailed alternately on both sides of the posts, so the fence looks the same from the neighbor's side. A vertical board-and-board fence (lower left) is another version of the same pattern. For an interesting change in the design, use fence boards of varying widths—either same-width boards in pairs or any combination you like.

Where a solid screen is unnecessary, an open-slat design is hard to beat. It breaks the wide-open feeling and allows good flow of air. For this fence variation, space 1x3 boards their own width apart. Secure the boards at the top, bottom, and middle. This simple fence design needs less lumber than others do.

A louver fence (lower right) offers both beauty and ventilation. Fence boards—usually 1x6s or 1x8s—are

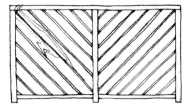
HERRINGBONE

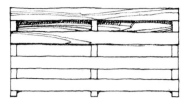
BOARD-AND-BOARD (horizontal)

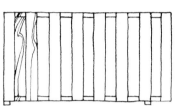
BOARD-AND-BOARD (vertical)

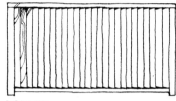
LOUVER

angled and overlap slightly. The degree of angle determines the degree of privacy.

Or you might try a handsome fence of alternating horizontal and vertical ½x5-inch louvers. Such a fence offers built-in privacy from street and neighbors, while allowing cooling breezes to pass through.

Construction Tips

• A privacy fence usually stands tall, so it needs to be sturdy. *How tall*

depends on your preference and the local building codes. Check with a building inspector for regulations, especially if you plan to build a privacy fence that will be higher than five feet.

• Also, have a surveyor check property lines to make sure your fence will be on your lot—not your neighbor's. Even after verifying your boundaries, it's best to build the fence six inches or so inside your lot

A privacy fence surrounds a formal garden, adding to its air of seclusion.

Six lattice panels combine for effective privacy, yet give an open feeling.

Specially detailed entries, like this one, extend a hearty welcome to visitors.

Plants set in panel holes filled with soil blossom to form a wall of flowers.

line in case of a faulty survey.

• When choosing materials, keep in mind that redwood and cedar are sturdy—and expensive—choices. Left untreated, they will weather to a soft, driftwood gray. Or you can stain or paint the wood.

The construction of your fence depends largely on the sturdiness of the posts you install. Choose posts that are large enough—usually 4x4s, sometimes 6x6s—and plant them firmly in the ground. The best method is to set posts in concrete to a depth exceeding the frost line in your part of the country. If you're not using redwood or cedar, the fence posts should be pressure-treated wood to resist rotting. Be sure each post stands straight (use a level and check two adjacent sides). Taper the tops of posts to shed water and prevent rot.

Set posts far enough apart to keep expenses down, but close enough to each other for proper support. Six feet between posts is usually about right. Use galvanized nails. Horizontal rails should join at posts—never in between.

Gates should be a minimum of three feet wide, with latches and hinges firmly attached to adjoining walls or posts.

This lofty, streetside utility screen offers privacy and provides the homeowner with raised planters.

Landscaping Ideas

Take that landscaping challenge and blend, disguise, or correct it with imagination and planning. Ideas presented here are only to plant the seed—or construct the screen, arrange the no-weed mulch, or splash the surroundings with color. Eyesores and imperfections often inspire clever design solutions.

design concept— front of ranch house

- ☐ expands scale of entrance
- ☐ creates sense of enclosure
- ☐ provides elements of interest to make the entrance more exciting

1 redbud

Cercis canadensis 30′

- ☐ flowers: purplish pink in May
- ☐ yellow fall color
- ☐ loose, informal shape
- ☐ defines space in court, provides canopy

2 wood screen

- ☐ gives partial enclosure; extends architecture to unify space

3 wood bench

- ☐ unifies design elements

4 wood edger 2x4 redwood

- ☐ provides crisp edge
- ☐ contains mulch material

5 purpleleaf winter creeper

Euonymus fortunei 'colorata'

- ☐ provides rich green carpet in entrance court
- ☐ mulch: bark, chips, or pea gravel
- ☐ leaves dark, deep purple above; paler beneath in autumn, winter

6 light/sculpture

- ☐ vertical element to add interest, scale, and light to entrance court

7 entrance court

- ☐ provides space for use as well as display
- ☐ different ground textures and patterns to give warmth (exposed aggregate and ground cover)

8 clay pots with annuals

- ☐ provide movable color

9 rhododendron 'P.J.M. Hybrids' 6′

- ☐ large, lavender-pink flowers
- ☐ broad-leaved evergreen—glossy foliage
- ☐ tender without winter mulch

ALTERNATE PLANT

- ☐ compact species of hydrangea

Landscaping as an art form

Texture. Are the leaves rough or smooth? Lacy or fuzzy? Shiny or dull? Textures are important when plants are placed near buildings, because contrasting textures emphasize or minimize architectural lines. Contrasts within groups of plants also can be part of the design. For example, the fine, feathery quality of juniper may be enhanced when placed beside a shiny, broad-leaved evergreen.

Color. Flowering plants can add sparkle to a landscape. But they are best used as accents rather than major components because their blooms are often brief and their foliage seldom striking. Plant them in large clumps.

Fragrance. Scent is one of the garden's most subtle delights. Roses, lilacs, and hyacinths are familiar. A mock orange close to an outdoor sitting area or gardenia bush beneath a bedroom window is a refreshing design inspiration. But don't stop with flowers. Many trees and herbs can be a treat to the nose, as well.

Character. What sets your favorite plants apart from others? These qualities give a plant character. Tamarisk, weeping willow, and columbine are delicate; oaks stately; lindens and aspens sparkling and gay; cedars and yews somber. Mixing plants of different characters can add up to visual chaos. Select plants in keeping with the character of your house, too. Think twice before using a flamboyant, exotic bush (suitable for a modern California ranch house) to frame a Cape Cod.

Harmony. Your landscape design can be a three-part harmony, just like your special tune. In music, it's the pleasing arrangement of notes; around your home, it's a combination of size, role, and eye level (or what you see when you look straight ahead). Large plants, trees for example, fix visual boundaries and provide canopy. Medium-size plants serve as screens while they also outline an area. Small ones, such as ground covers and flowers, supply color, pattern, and texture.

10 **Japanese tree lilac**
Syringa reticulata 30'
☐ creamy white flowers
☐ interesting bark

11 **quaking aspen**
Populus tremuloides 65'
☐ slender upright form
☐ light gray to white bark
☐ gold-yellow brilliant fall color
ALTERNATE PLANTS
☐ river birch
☐ black alder

12 **pachysandra**
Pachysandra terminalis 12''
☐ broad-leaved evergreen (white flower spikes in May)
☐ white berries
☐ dark green and lustrous
ALTERNATE PLANT
☐ periwinkle

13 **wood edger 2x4 redwood**
☐ outlines design

14 **precast concrete steppers**
☐ extend paving from entrance court to rear yard
☐ add interest to blank area

15 **mulch**
☐ pea gravel
☐ keeps area low-care

design concept—
front of colonial house

- ☐ creates warm, inviting entrance court
- ☐ uses plants to create framework for entrance, with lower plants used in a formal design to complement the architecture
- ☐ larger plants provide color and interest

1 sugar maple
Acer saccharum 80′

- ☐ tall, round form
- ☐ yellow-orange fall color

2 dorothea crab apple
Malus 'Dorothea'

- ☐ flowers—crimson to rose
- ☐ fruits—bright yellow
- ☐ dense, rounded habit
- ☐ provides soft transition from building to ground

3 saucer magnolia
Magnolia x soulangiana 25′

- ☐ one of the earliest plants to bloom
- ☐ large tulip-like flowers appear before leaves
- ☐ location of plant gives importance to house entrance
- ☐ annual pruning needed until desired canopy is reached

4 compact burning bush
Euonymus alata 'compacta'

- ☐ brilliant red fall color
- ☐ easy to maintain as formal hedge due to its slow to moderate growth—little trimming needed
- ☐ coarse branching structure with corky ridges on branches
- ☐ softens straight lines of walkway

ALTERNATE PLANTS

- ☐ barberry
- ☐ boxwood

5 purpleleaf winter creeper
Euonymus fortunei 'colorata'

- ☐ broad-leaved evergreen
- ☐ fall and winter color: purple

ALTERNATE PLANT

- ☐ periwinkle for shady situations

6 pagoda dogwood
Cornus alternifolia 15′

- ☐ unique horizontal branching
- ☐ small cream-colored flowers
- ☐ interesting winter branching pattern
- ☐ intended to reach over top of entrance door for shade and accent

7 dwarf Japanese yew
Taxus cuspidata 'nana'

- ☐ formal/traditional dark green
- ☐ evergreen plant
- ☐ easily maintained as a very thick formal hedge
- ☐ used as a continuous line to provide horizontal extension that appears to reduce height of house

ALTERNATE PLANT

- ☐ juniper for hot, exposed locations

8 brick surface

- ☐ entrance court is large enough to be in scale with house
- ☐ traditional theme

9 flower border

- ☐ adds a splash of color to entrance court

10 bigleaf winter creeper
Euonymus fortunei 'vegeta'

- ☐ semievergreen
- ☐ showy pink capsule with orange berrylike fruit
- ☐ used here to break starkness of chimney

ALTERNATE PLANT

- ☐ clematis

design concept—entrance with grade change

☐ provides smooth architectural extension of house entrance to drive

1 *cutleaf staghorn sumac*
Rhus typhina 'laciniata' 10'

☐ foliage: fine-textured, feathery

☐ fall color: bright orange red

☐ provides interesting textural quality to entrance

ALTERNATE PLANT

☐ smooth sumac

2 *creeping juniper*
Juniperus horizontalis

3 *retaining walls*
(railroad tie construction)

☐ provides crisp architectural grade transition from drive to entrance

☐ ties together architectural and natural elements of entrance

4 *recess this area from drive to facilitate easy access to and from auto*

5 *steps*

☐ grade transition with railroad ties

☐ steps and earth slope

6 *purpleleaf winter creeper*
Euonymus fortunei 'colorata'

☐ used here to hold slope

☐ attractive foliage

ALTERNATE PLANTS

☐ periwinkle

☐ creeping juniper

7 *radiant crab apple*
Malus 'Radiant' 25'

☐ flowers: deep pink, very showy

☐ fruits: bright red

☐ desired canopy obtained by pruning

☐ accents entrance, provides interest, interrupts roof line

ALTERNATE PLANTS

☐ other crab apple varieties

8 *bigleaf winter creeper*
Euonymus fortunei 'Sarcoxie'

☐ semievergreen

☐ showy pink capsule with orange berrylike fruit

☐ glossy green foliage

☐ will intertwine with ties

9 *rhododendron 'P.J.M. Hybrids' 6'*

☐ flower: bright lavender pink

☐ broad-leaved evergreen, foliage turns purple in fall

☐ provides splash of color at entrance

ALTERNATE PLANTS

☐ other varieties of rhododendron

10 *sargent juniper*
Juniperus chinensis 'sargenti'

☐ evergreen

☐ steel blue foliage

11 *common witch hazel*
Hamamelis virginiana 15'

☐ yellow flowers blooming in late fall

☐ fall color clear yellow

☐ excellent specimen for seasonal interest

☐ provides smooth transition from front to side of house

ALTERNATE PLANT

☐ star magnolia

More Options

Outdoor living areas become your little corner of the world. Backyards and garden corners greet you with soothing lines and cheerful colors, while permitting privacy and easy maintenance. Pay special attention to shapes and hues for a lovely view throughout the year.

design concept— a pleasant, private patio

☐ expands scale of existing patio with ground cover and concrete stepping-stones

☐ creates a sense of intimacy and enclosure with privacy screen and plant materials

1 creeping juniper
Juniperus horizontalis 12''

☐ foliage: bluish green to steel blue

☐ maintenance-free, low-growing mat

☐ well suited for hot, dry conditions

2 redbud
Cercis canadensis 30'

☐ branches lined with small pink-purple blossoms in early spring

☐ picturesque character with rounded form

☐ fall color: yellow

3 wood bench

☐ one end serves as planter

☐ unity between bench and planters

4 wood screen

☐ encloses space and adds privacy

☐ provides architectural extension of house

5 precast concrete stepping-stones

6 Mollis azalea

☐ flower: choice of several bright colors

☐ loses leaves in winter

☐ needs protection in cold climates

☐ grows best in well-drained soil, but must be kept moist

7 Japanese maple
Acer palmatum 20'

☐ foliage: green to red, fine-textured

☐ fall color: scarlet

☐ interesting form

☐ sturdy

8 wood planter boxes

☐ give vertical dimension to patio

☐ useful for bright flowers

☐ can be moved for new look or seasonal plant needs

9 purpleleaf winter creeper
Euonymus fortunei 'colorata' 12''

☐ easy to establish and maintain

☐ leaves turn a purple-red in autumn

10 wood edger

☐ maintains edge of planting spaces

11 Anthony Waterer spirea
Spiraea x bumalda

☐ maintains low, rounded form

☐ crimson flowers in flat-topped clusters

12 shadblow serviceberry (juneberry)
Amelanchier canadensis 60'

☐ vertical lines add height to horizontal architecture

☐ light gray bark

☐ fall colors: rich yellow and red

☐ needs little pruning or fertilizing

ALTERNATE PLANTS

☐ amur maple

☐ tatarian maple

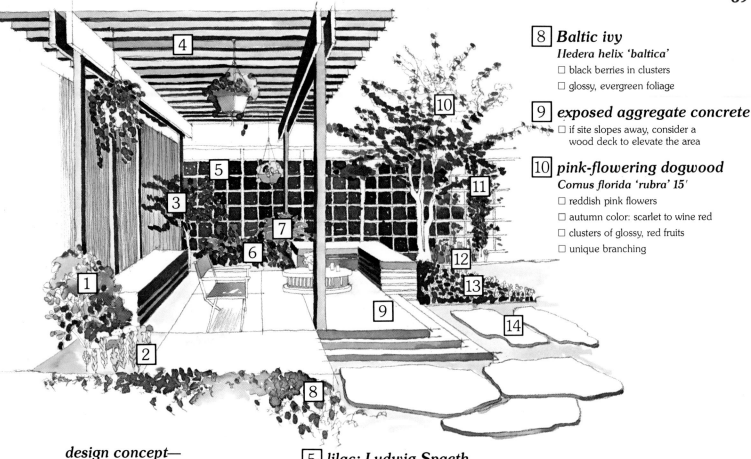

8 *Baltic ivy*
Hedera helix 'baltica'
- ☐ black berries in clusters
- ☐ glossy, evergreen foliage

9 *exposed aggregate concrete*
- ☐ if site slopes away, consider a wood deck to elevate the area

10 *pink-flowering dogwood*
Cornus florida 'rubra' 15'
- ☐ reddish pink flowers
- ☐ autumn color: scarlet to wine red
- ☐ clusters of glossy, red fruits
- ☐ unique branching

11 *jackman clematis vine*
Clematis x jackmani 12'
- ☐ large violet/purple flowers
- ☐ do best in partial shade
- ☐ prune to ground in dormant season

12 *tulips*
- ☐ a splash of seasonal color
- ☐ plant several varieties for blooms from early spring through early summer

13 *lily-of-the-valley*
Convallaria majalis
- ☐ rich, lustrous foliage
- ☐ prefers shade
- ☐ serves as a spring-flowering ground cover
- ☐ hardy

14 *stepping-stones*
- ☐ expands living space without "solid concrete" look
- ☐ free form fits soft lines of garden space

design concept—
a secluded garden corner
- ☐ creates a structured garden space with the help of plants

1 *bayberry*
Myrica pensylvanica 6'
- ☐ dull green, semievergreen foliage
- ☐ aromatic leaves
- ☐ wax-gray berries

2 *sedum autumn joy*
Sedum spectabile 'Autumn Joy' 16"
- ☐ flowers in late summer
- ☐ plant retains mushroom-shaped seed head through winter
- ☐ soft, light, moss-green leaves

3 *Japanese maple*
Acer palmatum 20'
- ☐ foliage: green to red, fine-textured
- ☐ adds a sculptural element to garden
- ☐ fall color: scarlet

4 *latticed wood sun screen*
- ☐ gives overhead definition to space
- ☐ provides interesting shadow patterns

5 *lilac: Ludwig Spaeth*
Syringa vulgaris 'Ludwig Spaeth'
- ☐ used as hedge behind lattice
- ☐ deep purple flowers
- ☐ lovely scent
ALTERNATE PLANT
- ☐ Zabeli honeysuckle

6 *Korean azalea*
Rhododendron yedoense 'poukhanense'
- ☐ flower: bright lavender-pink in early spring
- ☐ hardy in North
- ☐ broad-leaved evergreen in South

7 *spreading cotoneaster*
Cotoneaster divaricatus 6'
- ☐ small pink flowers
- ☐ bright red fruit in fall
- ☐ fall color: dull red
- ☐ arching, spreading habit
- ☐ pruned and developed as garden specimen
ALTERNATE PLANT
- ☐ pyracantha

design concept—
a narrow display garden
between house and driveway

☐ narrow space developed as a
summer display garden

☐ year-round appeal of area achieved with ground
cover and posts

1 *Katherine crab apple*

Malus 'Katherine' 20'

☐ flowers: large, double, pink to white

☐ small red fruits

☐ used here to terminate garden and to
soften corner of house

2 *wood posts of varying heights*

☐ pleasant surprises rising from ground cover

☐ discarded telephone poles, railroad ties,
or tree rounds—buried in ground at least
1½ feet, deeper for higher posts

3 *giant allium*

Allium giganteum

☐ six- to eight-inch round purple flowers
(from bulb) on five- to seven-foot stems

☐ a specimen

☐ for summer color: geraniums (sun)
impatiens or caladiums (shade)

4 *purpleleaf winter creeper*

Euonymus fortunei 'colorata' 12''

☐ carpets areas between display posts

☐ semievergreen to evergreen

☐ turns purple in fall

ALTERNATE PLANT

☐ periwinkle

5 *clay tile or crockery*

☐ larger elements provide
scale and balance in the composition

6 *clay pots with seasonal*
flowers—geraniums, petunias,
and mums

☐ pots of various sizes and styles
must harmonize

☐ ideal for summering
houseplants, if area is shaded

☐ use one or two for herbs—pots
can later be moved inside

design concept—
back door beautification
- ☐ makes an otherwise dull entrance a pleasant and convenient feature

1 *daphne spirea*
Spiraea japonica 'alpina' 12''
- ☐ flowers: light pink masses in spring— intermittent blossoms throughout summer

ALTERNATE PLANTS
- ☐ creeping juniper 'Blue Rug' (sun)
- ☐ pachysandra (shade)

2 *mulch*
- ☐ bark chunks or gravel
- ☐ contained by edger or existing walk

3 *shelf*
- ☐ adds interest to a plain house
- ☐ a handsome setting for potted plants

4 *Korean spice viburnum*
Viburnum carlesi 5'
- ☐ flowers: pink to white with spicy fragrance
- ☐ small black berries attract birds
- ☐ foliage: wine red in autumn

ALTERNATE PLANTS
- ☐ rhododendron
- ☐ Japanese quince

5 *wood platform*
- ☐ expands feeling of space at entrance
- ☐ handy for outdoor cooking

6 *space frame*
- ☐ an architectural extension of entrance
- ☐ a place for summer potted plants
- ☐ firewood storage rack below

7 *harbinger European bird cherry (mayday tree)*
Prunus padus 'commutata' 30'
- ☐ blooms in early May
- ☐ flowers: small, white clusters
- ☐ for scale and space definition

ALTERNATE PLANTS
- ☐ pagoda dogwood
- ☐ Japanese tree lilac

8 *back door mini garden*
- ☐ for bright annuals and bulbs
- ☐ 30-inch water saucer for birds
- ☐ wood-edger-defined bed
- ☐ birdhouse in tree above

Know Your Soil

Good soil is important to the growing success of your new landscape plantings. And if you find you don't have ideal—or even good—soil, you don't have to be satisfied with what you have. You can improve it to help ensure that your plants feel at home. Here's how.

Gardening is like most hobbies in that you can get as involved as you like. No one is going to say you must thoroughly understand the soil or how plants grow in order to enjoy your garden. If you're at all serious about gardening, though, there are a few things you should know about your soil.

Most garden publications will tell you an ideal garden soil is deep, friable, fertile, well-drained, and high in organic matter. Don't be disappointed if your soil doesn't fit that description. Few garden soils do.

If you find the soil to be less than ideal, you can either leave it as is or try to improve it. Before you start making changes, find out what you have. And even if you decide not to make changes, getting to know your soil will help you decide what plants will grow best on your lot.

In getting to know your soil, you'll need to understand certain physical and chemical characteristics. Physical characteristics include the soil's composition, texture, structure, depth, and drainage. The main chemical characteristics you'll need to be aware of include the pH and the overall fertility level.

Composition. Soil is composed of four primary materials—sand, clay, silt, and organic matter (humus). The type of soil you have and many of its characteristics are determined by the proportion of

these four materials present.

The composition of your soil is related to soil texture and soil structure. It is important to know something about the composition of the soil if you attempt to adjust the pH or apply chemicals to your garden, because recommendations generally vary according to soil type. Knowing something about your soil's composition will also give you an idea of how well it will hold fertility and how well it will drain.

Although it would take a laboratory analysis to determine the exact proportions of sand, silt, clay, and organic matter in your soil, you can get a good idea what they are by observing the soil when you work it and by feeling its texture.

The two types that probably would give you the most problems are soils with too much clay and soils with too much sand.

A soil high in clay tends to be sticky. It will stick to your shovel when you're working it. And when it's moist, you can easily squeeze a clayey soil into a tight ball.

Soils with too much clay can cause problems for the gardener because they tend to be wet and difficult to work. Clay particles are small and fit closely together, leaving extremely small pores for air and water. On the other hand, your soil needs some clay to give it strength and water-holding capacity.

Soils with a high proportion of sand are nearly the opposite. The particles—and the spaces between them—are much larger, so sandy soils are crumbly in texture. If you try to squeeze a handful of your soil into a ball and it always crumbles apart, you have a sandy soil.

Sandy soils are commonly called light soils—and they're very easy to work. They cause problems for gardeners, though, because water and plant nutrients move through them too quickly.

The term *soil texture* is closely related to soil composition in that it refers to the size of the soil particles. Texture depends on the relative amounts of sand, silt, and clay in the soil and influences porosity, water-holding capacity, drainage, and soil atmosphere.

Soil texture should influence the way you manage your garden. For

If you pick up a handful of your soil and can squeeze it into a tight, sticky mass, your soil is likely high in clay.

A loose, crumbly soil like that above won't hold any shape. This soil has a high sand content and won't retain moisture.

Soil of the proper texture will mold into your hand—yet crumble apart when squeezed.

example, if you have a fine-textured clay or silt soil, you need to be especially careful that you don't work the soil when it is too wet.

The term *soil structure* describes how soil particles are grouped and arranged. Structure also may influence porosity, water-holding capacity, drainage, and soil atmosphere. If soil is crumbly and somewhat porous, but not too lumpy, it has good structure. Adding organic matter (humus-making materials) may improve structure.

Depth. The root zone of plants is wider and deeper than most gardeners realize, so you want a soil that is deep enough to accommodate it. Because roots grow best in topsoil, that soil should be as deep as possible.

Drainage. Soil drainage is important because soil occasionally receives more water than it needs. Plant roots need air as well as water, so if all the soil's pores are filled with water, your plants will suffer. A poorly drained soil often will be too wet and cold for proper plant growth.

Chemical characteristics. Soils have chemical reactions going on all the time, but the only chemical characteristics you need to know about are the pH (the acidity-alkalinity relationship) and the overall level of fertility. The only sure way to determine your soil's pH and fertility is with a soil test. Color, soil texture, and other physical characteristics should not be used to indicate soil fertility.

Soil testing

The only accurate way to determine the levels of various nutrients in your soil—and to find out what percentage of those nutrients will become available to plants during the next growing season—is to take a soil test.

Many gardeners think soil testing only determines the soil's pH, but, through it, you also can find out what nutrients are present. Standard soil tests will tell you the pH of your soil, how much phosphorus and potassium are available, and how much organic matter the soil contains. If you think you might have a problem, tests also are avail-

able that give you a complete report on the other essential elements.

The first step in soil testing is to get a good, representative sample of the soil in your garden. Take samples from different areas by digging to a depth of six to eight inches and taking a thin slice of soil from the edge of the hole. Mix the samples thoroughly to obtain about a half-pint of soil as your final sample.

Remove roots, sticks, or stones from the sample, and keep it in a clean, dry, covered container until it's tested. If you have several kinds of soil in your garden, you may want to take separate samples.

Once you have a sample, your local county extension office can tell you where to send it. Most states operate soil testing services that charge a small fee (perhaps $3 to $5 per sample) for their work.

If you want to get involved yourself, buy a soil testing kit and do your own tests. Remember that your results may not be quite so accurate as those from a standardized laboratory.

The final, and most important, step in soil testing is interpreting the results. The most accurate soil test will do you little good if it's interpreted poorly.

More and more state extension services are developing special interpretations and recommendations for tests of lawn and garden samples. In some cases, the recommendations are even computerized. Those you receive will tell how much lime you should add to adjust the pH and how much phosphorus and potassium you should add to bring these elements up to acceptable levels.

Nitrogen recommendations generally are not based on the soil test, because the element moves through the soil so quickly that the amount of nitrogen changes.

Making changes

Once you know what your soil is like, you're ready to try some improvements. Your changes can be as simple as tilling the soil, or as complex as establishing a complete composting system.

Proper tillage can go a long way toward improving the structure

of your soil. On the other hand, improper tillage can do your garden some harm.

Never till your soil when it's too wet. Take a handful of soil and squeeze it together. If it forms a sticky, compact mess, then it's too wet to be worked. Heavy clay soils that are tilled when they're too wet become hard and lumpy.

Even when moisture content is right, it's possible to overwork your soil. You don't want to work it so finely that it will crust after a rain. You want to break up the clods and level the surface, but not destroy the soil structure.

Soil amendments. If you find it necessary to improve the physical structure of your soil, there are a number of approaches you can use successfully. If you have a heavy clay soil, you might consider adding some sand to it for improved drainage and workability. Or if you have a light sandy soil, you might consider mixing in some clay to improve the texture.

A more common approach to improving your soil's physical characteristics is to add organic matter like compost or peat. Such materials can go a long way toward improving your soil's structure.

Humus sometimes is called a cure-all for every soil weakness. If you add humus to sandy soil, you'll get improved water retention; add it to a clay soil, and the soil will be more friable and easily worked. If you till it deeply into heavy soil, you will get improved drainage. And, if it's added regularly over a period of years, humus will improve the fertility of any soil.

There are several types of humus-producing organic materials available. Among these are manure, compost, peat moss, sewage sludge, sawdust, and straw. If these materials are applied over a period of several years, there always should be enough humus decaying to supply your soil with a certain amount of plant nutrients. However, because none of these materials contains very many plant nutrients, they should not be substituted for fertilizer.

Try to incorporate organic matter into the soil in the fall to give the microorganisms in the soil a chance

to decompose the material in advance of spring planting.

It's also a good idea to incorporate about two pounds of 10-10-10 fertilizer per 100 square feet. The microorganisms that decompose the organic matter get their energy from plant nutrients, so if you don't add the fertilizer, they tie up essential elements during the decomposition process, elements that are then unavailable to plants.

You may see chemical soil amendments on the market whose makers claim they will improve the structure of your soil and increase your yields. Be sure to check carefully before buying such products. Soil scientists have tested many such products, and have found few (if any) that have a significant effect on soils and plant growth.

Fertilizers. The easiest method of improving soil fertility is through the addition of chemical fertilizers. Unfortunately, fertilizers can be expensive, so it makes good sense to apply them only as needed.

Plants need at least 16 elements for healthy growth. Only four of them commonly are applied as fertilizer—nitrogen, phosphorus, potassium, and calcium. Plants also use large amounts of carbon, hydrogen, and oxygen—elements they get from air and water—as well as sulfur and magnesium.

The elements needed in smaller quantities—called *micronutrients* —include iron, manganese, zinc, copper, molybdenum, boron, and chlorine. Although micronutrients are needed in smaller quantities, they're important. These elements are generally present in soils, but in some parts of the country, one or more of them may be deficient.

Your soil's pH. The pH scale is used as an index of your soil's acidity or alkalinity. Plants differ, but most can tolerate a fairly wide range of pH values.

Most garden plants thrive when the pH is between 6 and 7 (close to neutral) and grow reasonably well with a pH between 5.5 and 7.2. If you find your soil has a lower pH (too acid), you will need to add hydrated lime or pulverized limestone to neutralize it. Be sure to follow soil test recommendations in deciding how much to add.

Plant Foods: How to Choose and Use

How to choose plant foods depends on the objectives you have for your lawn or plants. If you simply want to keep them alive, a yearly application of a complete fertilizer should do the trick. But if you want your plants to do their best, you'll need to do more.

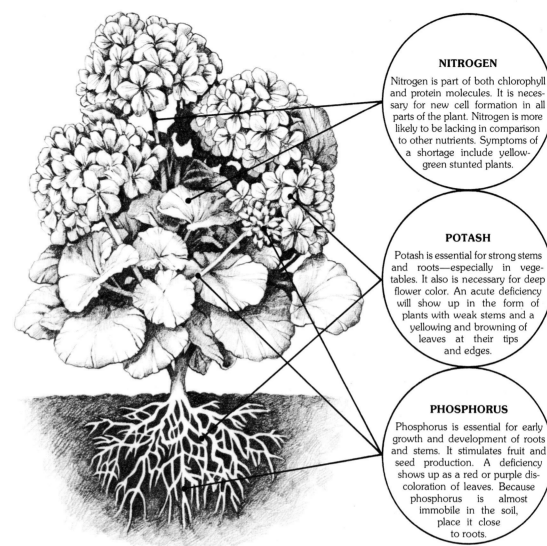

NITROGEN

Nitrogen is part of both chlorophyll and protein molecules. It is necessary for new cell formation in all parts of the plant. Nitrogen is more likely to be lacking in comparison to other nutrients. Symptoms of a shortage include yellow-green stunted plants.

POTASH

Potash is essential for strong stems and roots—especially in vegetables. It also is necessary for deep flower color. An acute deficiency will show up in the form of plants with weak stems and a yellowing and browning of leaves at their tips and edges.

PHOSPHORUS

Phosphorus is essential for early growth and development of roots and stems. It stimulates fruit and seed production. A deficiency shows up as a red or purple discoloration of leaves. Because phosphorus is almost immobile in the soil, place it close to roots.

Of the 16 nutrients essential to plant growth and reproduction, soils are likely to be deficient in only four: nitrogen, phosphorus, potassium, and calcium. The first three are included in mixed, commercial fertilizers, but calcium is usually sold separately in the form of limestone.

The best way to know how much and in what proportion to add plant nutrients is with a soil test. State agricultural agencies and some local nurseries can test your soil. Simply take them soil samples from a number of spots in your yard, especially where new plants will go.

Once a soil test indicates what nutrients you need to add, you can select a fertilizer to correct most of those deficiencies.

As you become more involved in managing your soil, you will probably hear a good deal about the benefits of one type of fertilizer as compared with another. In weighing these arguments, remember that plants can't distinguish between the sources of their nutrients. Plants simply need to have all of the nutrients present in sufficient quantities, in the proper proportions, and in a form they can use.

The key to nutrient value is availability. Fertilizer needs to be soluble and available to plants soon after application. Soil elements such as phosphorus and potassium—even though plentiful in the soil—can become fixed to soil particles so they are not available to plants.

Organic plant foods include compost, manure, sewage sludge, bonemeal, tankage, blood meal, cottonseed meal, and soybean meal. If you are planning to buy any of these materials, remember that their nutrient analysis—in terms of nitrogen, phosphorus, and potash—is low, so the nutrients you buy may be more expensive than if you bought them in one of the inorganic fertilizers. You should also be sure to consider some other characteristics of organic plant foods as you make your selection. Except for bonemeal, nitrogen is the predominant nutrient in plant foods. They usually contain less phosphorus and potash. In bonemeal, phosphorus predominates. The nutrients in organic plant foods are insoluble and become available only as the material decays in the soil. That makes them slow-acting and long-lasting. And finally, organic fertilizers alone are not balanced sources of the nutrients your soil needs.

Inorganic plant foods are either mined or manufactured and have characteristics that contrast strongly with organic fertilizers. Their nutrients are in soluble form so they are quickly available to plants but are not very long-lasting. Their solubility can make them caustic to plants. If you apply them in concentrated amounts, be careful to keep them from direct contact with roots and foliage or you might kill the plants. Analysis of chemical fertilizers is relatively high in terms of the nutrients they contain.

The ratio of nutrients contained in fertilizer must be printed directly on the container. The numbers indicate the percentage of nitrogen, phosphorus, and potash, in that order. Thus, a 12-12-12 fertilizer contains 12 percent, by weight, of each nutrient; the rest is inert matter.

Because of the different characteristics of organic and inorganic

PLANT	SEASON TO FEED	SPECIAL NOTES
Annuals	Before planting	Spread food before turning soil for bed. Feed again when plants are thinned
Bulbs, tubers	Early spring or fall	Add food to planting pocket, either complete plant food or superphosphate
Evergreens	Early spring	Feed sheared ones again in fall. Use "acid" foods for azaleas, camellias
Fruit trees	Fall or spring	Use supplementary nitrogen in early spring in addition to yearly feeding
Hedges	Spring	Feed sheared hedges again in fall
Houseplants	Any time	Feed sparingly every two or three months except during winter when plants cease active growth
Lawns	Spring and fall	Supply extra nitrogen in fall if grass is damaged by drought or hard use
Perennials	When growth starts	Repeat when flower buds appear
Roses	Spring and summer	Fall feeding may force new growth that will be damaged by cold
Shrubs	Spring or fall	One feeding a year usually sufficient for mature plants
Small fruits	Spring or fall	Two feedings a year preferred for most bramble fruits. Extra summer feeding may increase crop
Trees	Spring	Repeat in fall if tree is weak, or damaged by drought, disease, or insects
Vegetables	Planting time	Side-dress when plants are thinned, or shortly after thinning. Check instructions on specially formulated vegetable foods
Vines	Spring or fall	Feed both spring and fall until plants get well established, then once a year

fertilizers, many gardeners find a combination of the two produces the best results. Cost and available supplies may influence your choice.

Fertilizer forms. Liquid plant foods have no particular advantage over the dry forms, except around individual plants or for use as starter solutions. They're also good for accurate application to houseplants and other container-grown plants.

Slow-release fertilizers, such as sulphur-coated urea, work on the same principle as the "time" capsules you take for your cold—they feed the plants slowly over an extended period. Slow-release fertilizers are especially useful on lawns because you can apply them at high rates and not burn the grass. They

also save time because you don't have to repeat applications often.

A complete fertilizer is one that has all three major nutrients. The nutrients in any particular fertilizer may not be in the proper balance or ratio for your needs. Look for a fertilizer that contains nitrogen, phosphorus, and potassium in the approximate ratio recommended by the soil test. Then base your rate of application on the recommendations provided by the soil test.

Micronutrients. Some fertilizers contain a small quantity of certain micronutrients. But, because you usually must pay extra for micronutrients in fertilizers, it is best not to apply them unless you find your plants have serious growing

problems and a soil test shows one or more micronutrients to be in short supply. Because these elements are generally needed in such small amounts, any excess can be toxic to most of the plants.

Limestone should only be applied if a soil test indicates your soil is too acidic and you need to raise the pH. Soils with a pH of 6.5 to 7.0 will support the growth of most garden plants. (Do not add limestone without first having a soil test.)

Applying plant foods

Applying plant foods most effectively requires you to know when your

plants need the nutrients, how quickly the nutrients become available from the fertilizer you select, and which fertilizer placement will be most beneficial.

The chart at the left summarizes when you should fertilize various types of plants. In determining the proper fertilizer placement, it helps to realize that phosphorus and potassium are fairly immobile once in the soil. As a result, they need to be placed near the root zone of the plants you're trying to feed. With these two elements especially, it does little good to spread fertilizer on top of the ground and hope it will work its way to the root zone.

Broadcasting fertilizer with a mechanical spreader is the best way to cover large areas. If you garden and want to add nutrients to the soil, it's best to broadcast fertilizer in the fall or spring, before planting. Then work the fertilizer into the top two or three inches of soil.

Starter solutions are best used when transplanting large plants such as tomatoes. You can buy a commercial preparation or mix your own by dissolving one cup of 5-10-5 or 5-10-10 in three gallons of water. Pour this around the roots as the planting hole is filled until the soil is thoroughly moistened.

Side-dressing is a way of adding needed nutrients during the growing season. Spread the fertilizer in a row at least six inches from the base of the plants, letting the band extend eight to 12 inches away from the row.

Deep feeding is usually not necessary to get nutrients down to the roots of trees and shrubs. Use a water lance with tree food only for young trees. The majority of a tree's feeder roots—the ones that can use nutrients—are located in the top ten to 12 inches of soil, so deep feeding is not required. Check with your local arborist or county extension office for help analyzing your trees' needs.

Base feeding. For roses and shrubs, begin fertilizing six to 12 inches from the plant, and extend the circle of plant food six to 12 inches beyond the branch tips. Scratch the fertilizer into the soil, but be sure to be careful so you don't damage shallow roots.

Consider Your Climate

With the information from the temperature zone map at right, you can learn the approximate range of minimum temperatures in all parts of the country, and more particularly in your area. Use this map to help choose the right plants for your garden.

The climate in your area is a mixture of many different weather patterns: sun, snow, rain, wind, humidity. To be a good gardener, you should know, on an average, how cold the garden gets in winter, how much rainfall it receives each year, and how hot or dry it becomes in a typical summer. You can obtain this general information from your state agricultural school or your county extension agent. In addition, acquaint yourself with the mini-climates in your own neighborhood, based on such things as wind protection gained from a nearby hill, or humidity and cooling offered by a local lake or river.

Then carry the research further by studying the microclimates that characterize your own plot of ground. Land on the south side of your house is bound to be warmer than a constantly shaded area exposed to cold, northwest winds. An area in the full, hot sun is generally drier than· a depression along a drainage route.

Watch how the snow piles up in the garden. Drifts supplying valuable extra water may be caused by the shape of the house or a deflection of wind around a high fence or wall. Study the length of tree shadows in winter and summer and use the information to avoid disappointments. All these findings can help you decide what to plant and where to grow it best.

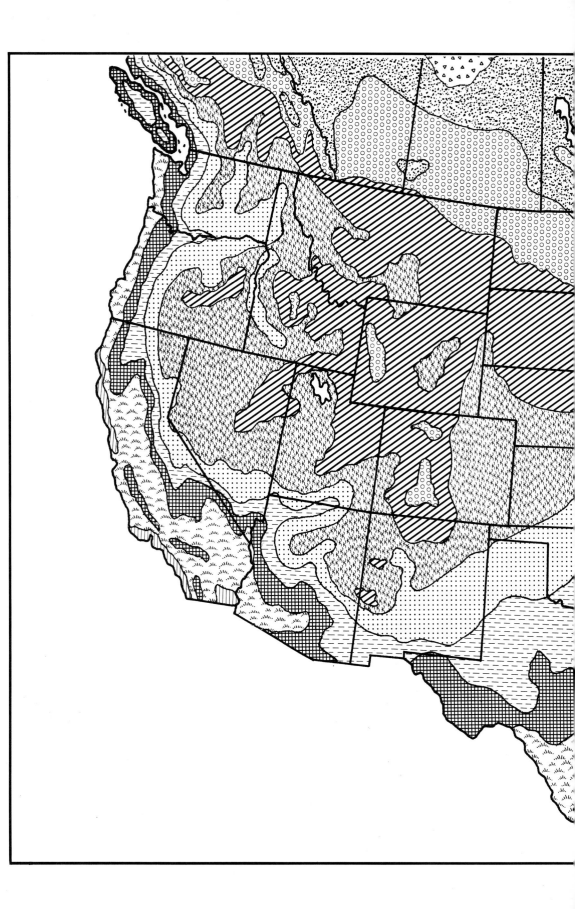

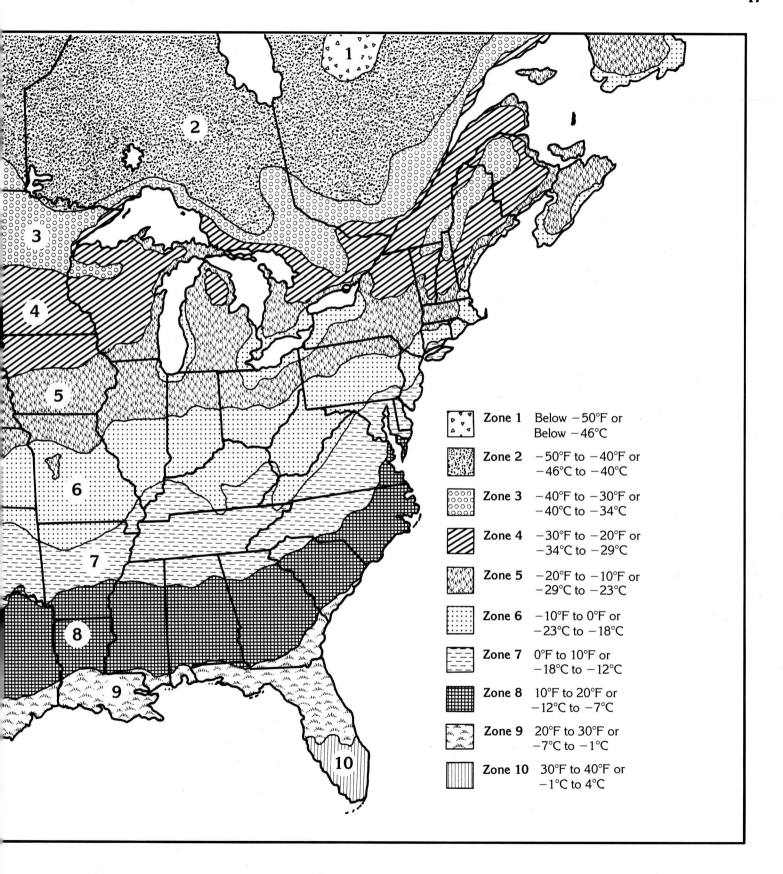

Zone 1 Below −50°F or Below −46°C

Zone 2 −50°F to −40°F or −46°C to −40°C

Zone 3 −40°F to −30°F or −40°C to −34°C

Zone 4 −30°F to −20°F or −34°C to −29°C

Zone 5 −20°F to −10°F or −29°C to −23°C

Zone 6 −10°F to 0°F or −23°C to −18°C

Zone 7 0°F to 10°F or −18°C to −12°C

Zone 8 10°F to 20°F or −12°C to −7°C

Zone 9 20°F to 30°F or −7°C to −1°C

Zone 10 30°F to 40°F or −1°C to 4°C

INDEX